Getting on With the Going

Fourth Printing
Revised

Joe Garner Turman

Getting on With the Going

Joe Garner Turman

PUBLISHED BY:
BRENTWOOD CHRISTIAN PRESS
4000 BEALLWOOD AVENUE
COLUMBUS, GEORGIA 31904

Dedication

To

My dear wife, Gloria, who started this marvelous missionary journey with me and has been a loving and faithful companion all along the way. Her encouragement and support was vital in every stage of our missionary ministry, and in my writing our missionary story.

to

Our children: Joey, Anne-Marie, Elizabeth and John Mark who are our favorite MKs. They, along with our daughter-in-law, Stephanie, and son-in-law, John Gabriel, have been a source of encouragement and practical help in our ministry, and in writing this book. Our grandchildren: Gabe, Kaitlin, Luke, Zachary, Claire and Nate who are willing to hear my stories. To them, I pass on the torch.

To

Southern Baptists who have loved us, prayed for us and supported us financially.

"I journeyed with Joe and Gloria through their mission fields. Joe's story-telling ability held my interest on every page and he made me feel the Holy Spirit's leadership without "spiritualizing. ""

Stuart Calvert, President, WMU Alabama

"Getting on With The Going is an excellent autobiography of a real, live missionary. Each page is alive, engaging and encouraging. You'll not want to put the book down until you have absorbed every word of it."

Bill Roberson, Missionary Emeritus,
IMB, Vietnam and Philippines

"Never has a true story touched lives as does the mission story of Joe and Gloria Turman. Their story is a read that cannot be put down, and their lives are a testimony of what God can do with obedient people."

Rev. Burgie Thompson, Pastor
Unity Baptist Church, Hugo, OK

"The Lord gave Joe and Gloria Turman the privilege of carrying the Gospel to the ends of the earth. Now we can read about this exciting adventure. Those who have supported missions can be thankful for a job well done. Read and be rewarded!"

Rev. Bob Connerley, Pastor,
Brownsville Baptist Church, Brownsville, TN

"A tremendously informative and exciting book about how God used Joe and Gloria Turman in mission work all over the world."

Randall Stoner, Director of Missions,
Marshall Baptist Association, Alabama

"It's great! I especially enjoyed the parts on Vietnam and Indonesia. I am challenged by the passion and perseverance for doing personal evangelism as modeled by the Turmans."

**Eric Dooley, Pastor,
New Life Fellowship, Ho Chi Minh City, Vietnam**

"Getting on With The Going is interesting, moving, compelling and challenging. I could not put it down until I had finished reading it. You cannot read this book without having a greater love for missions and our missionaries!"

**Max Roden, Pastor Gilliam
Springs Baptist Church, Arab, AL**

"Getting on With The Going is a heart touching story of a missionary journey by a family called out for this purpose. This book is written in a way that puts you right in the center of what God was doing on this journey. This book will bring us back to a real commitment to missions!"

**Otis Cayton Director of
Missions Frisco Baptist Association, Hugo, OK**

"I truly enjoyed reading *Getting on With The Going!* I felt like I was in the room listening to Brother Joe tell each story. I am amazed at God's providential provision for our missionaries."

Linda Henry, CWJC Coordinator Alabama WMU

"Joe and Gloria's adventures and lifestyle put in concrete exciting terms the kind of missionary needed for the future–mobile, passionate, enthusiastic, flexible, fearless and on the move. This fast moving book is a page turner as the Turmans move from one challenge to another on mission with God."

**Avery Willis
Emeritus, IMB Vice-President**

5

Table of Contents

From Darkness to Light

Getting out of a double-feature movie I wandered aimlessly about Times Square. It was a beautiful evening in May 1957. Since I had only two dollars left from my previous paycheck, I could not afford to spend any more money. The remaining money would have to be used for subway fare in going back and forth to work.

Walking down to Forty-ninth Street and Eighth Avenue, I saw hundreds of people entering Madison Square Garden. Many were carrying Bibles. Turning aside to see this unusual sight (people carrying Bibles), I glanced up at the marquee. The evening program was highlighted: Billy Graham Crusade, 1,500 Voice Choir, Free. The word "free" stopped me.

Joining the crowd of people entering Madison Square Garden, I found a seat on the top balcony. The people around me were friendly and smiling. Cliff Barrows led the congregation in singing several gospel songs. As I sang along with the crowd, a warm feeling swept over me. I remembered singing these songs in the Noonday Baptist Church at Noonday, Texas.

Mama and Papa had brought us up in church, but, in high school I begin to have other priorities. Playing football for Tyler High took a lot of my time and energy. After graduating from high school, I joined the Marines. Receiving an honorable discharge after a three-year tour of duty, I returned to my hometown. Feeling restless and dissatisfied with life in my home community, I traveled about Texas.

On a construction job in South Texas, I met Jimmy Leahy. Jimmy and I were the same age, twenty-two. Jimmy, like myself, was recently discharged from the armed forces, and was wandering about the country.

One day on the job, he suggested that we go to New York City where workers were paid higher wages. Jimmy had grown up in New York City.

We quit our job and went to the Big Apple. I found a job mixing drinks in the cocktail lounge, on the third floor, of Schraff's restaurant on Fifth Avenue. Jimmy found a job out in Queens.

Now after living for years in the far country as a prodigal son, I was about to be confronted by the convicting and converting power of the living Savior, Jesus Christ.

The 1,500-voice choir with George Beverly Shea sang "How Great Thou Art." Then, Billy Graham stood to deliver the message. I fixed my attention on this preacher from North Carolina. New York was buzzing with news about the crusade in the Garden. The newspapers, radios, TV programs and cabbies were all talking about Billy Graham. Some were wondering if he could defeat the Devil in the Garden. I was curious about his message.

I did not have to wait long! Billy Graham's message flowed in an eloquent, yet easy to understand style. His piercing eyes and Bible-centered preaching that was empowered by the Holy Spirit quickly commanded the attention of the 20,000 people.

Listening attentively, I began to feel uncomfortable. I ceased to be entertained as the Holy Spirit began a work of conviction in my heart. Standing up to leave, I could not, as my feet seemed to be riveted to the floor. I sat back down to continue to listen to the message. The Holy Spirit lifted up Jesus Christ. I saw Him dying on the cross for my sins...taking my place. For the first time in my life, I was impacted with what Jesus did for me, and others, on the cross. At that moment I realized how much God loved me.

During the invitation I bowed my head. Oblivious to anyone else's presence, I prayed, "Lord Jesus, I've made a mess out of my life. Please forgive me. Come into my life, Lord Jesus. I want to start over again. Come in and be my Lord and Savior!"

After that prayer of repentance and commitment, I felt a warm joy sweeping over me. The burden and weight of sin was lifted. I was free!

Suddenly, I wanted to tell everyone that Jesus is real. Along with hundreds of others, I made my way down to the front of the podium to publicly confess Jesus as Lord and Savior.

Coming out of Madison Square Garden, I headed for 42nd Street and Broadway where I would catch a subway back to my rented room in Queens.

Approaching 42nd Street and Broadway, I came upon a crowd of people surrounding a young man preaching the Gospel. Some in the crowd were throwing spitballs at him and others were cursing him. The young man had, evidently, just finished his message and was calling for a response, saying, "Who will step out for Jesus? Come and stand beside me."

The Lord spoke to me in such a clear way that I was startled: "Step out!" I immediately pushed my way through the crowd and stood with the young man.

That was the first time I was called upon to take a stand for Christ in hostile circumstances. In days ahead, there would be other opportunities to stand for Christ in hostile environments.

After arriving at my room, I sat down and wrote my Mom a letter telling her that I had given my life to Christ. I knew that she had been praying for me.

The next day I told the manager of the restaurant that I was quitting my job. I felt a need to get away from NYC to

11

a quieter and more peaceful atmosphere. Since my departure would create a vacancy that would need to be filled immediately, he asked me to work another week until he could train someone to take my place. I agreed to do so.

At the end of the week, I left New York saying goodbye to Jimmy and the rest of my friends and boarded a bus bound for St. Petersburg, Florida. I had often visited St. Pete while I was stationed in Florida as a Marine. The pleasant, slow-paced lifestyle that characterized the city appealed to me.

After my arrival in St. Pete, I rented a room in a private home owned by a widow from Nashville.

Looking over the newspaper ads, I found a job with a construction company building a power plant on Weedon Island. It was hard work, but I enjoyed it.

Several weeks later, I joined the Fifth Avenue Baptist Church where there was an active program for young people. Dr. Vaughn Johnson, the pastor, preached Biblical messages. My Sunday School teacher, a local businessman, taught the Scriptures in a creative and relevant way. The Bible came alive to me! Each week I could hardly wait to get to the next church service.

Calling, Commitment and Counting the Cost

Sitting under Biblical teaching and preaching, I was impacted with the truth that God wants to use every believer to bear witness to the saving power of Jesus Christ. This truth, working in my life, led to my calling and commitment to sharing the Good News.

Walking on Spar Beach, one Sunday afternoon, I started thinking about how I had wasted so much of my life in living to please myself. I began to see and to feel the lostness of the world. Suddenly, I sensed the burden of a lost world placed upon me. It was so heavy and overpowering that I literally could not stand.

Kneeling on the beach, I committed myself to the Lord Jesus, "Lord, I give myself to telling others about You."

Rising from my knees I felt a deep sense of joy and peace. I knew that what I did in that moment pleased the Lord. From that time on, I experienced a new sense of purpose in my life. I began to ask other young people about preparation for Christian service. I found out that there were fifteen students from Carson-Newman College in our church. Some of them were preparing for a Christian vocation.

Finding out that Carson-Newman was in Jefferson City, Tennessee, I wrote the registrar asking about possible enrollment. After sending the necessary information I waited to hear from the college.

At the time when the students from Carson-Newman were getting ready to return to the campus, I had not received any word from the school. Although I had not been accepted, I felt strongly that I should attend Carson-Newman. So, I quit my job, bought some clothes, a bus ticket and left for Tennessee.

Arriving on campus after a long, tiring trip, I went to the Admissions Office. They told me that my transcript from my high school in Texas had not come, thus I would need to come back in January.

I demurred, "I've come all the way from St. Petersburg, Florida and I can't go back. God has led me here."

Such an unexpected statement startled the administrators. They looked at one another. One of them said, "Excuse us for a moment."

They went into an office to discuss my situation. Coming back, they said, "You can stay in the transit room over in the Barn while you wait to see if your transcript will come on time for you to enroll."

The Barn was the oldest dormitory on campus where the athletes stayed. I was happy to have a place to lay my head.

After four days in the transit room, my high school transcript arrived in time for me to enroll. Without the sympathetic help of two administrators I would not have made the enrollment deadline. My enrollment was nothing short of a miracle.

At the end of my sophomore year, a fellow student asked me if I was interested in pastoring two small mission churches in Jamestown, Tennessee. I told him that I had very little experience, but I was willing to give it a try. The next Sunday I went to Jamestown and preached at the Round Mountain Baptist Mission and the Pine Haven Baptist Mission. Later on in the week the missions called and invited me to be their pastor.

The following week was the summer break. The Winningham family, at Round Mountain, which is just outside of Jamestown, invited me to stay with them for the summer. It was a memorable summer of visiting the lost, preaching, teaching, witnessing and learning some of the fundamentals of being a pastor.

Serving as pastor of Round Mountain and Pine Haven Baptist Missions (they later organized into churches) was a special and important time in my life of ministry. Even though I had more zeal than knowledge, the people loved me and supported me. I served as their pastor until I graduated and left to attend seminary in Texas.

In the fall of 1962, I enrolled in Southwestern Baptist Theological Seminary at Fort Worth, Texas. During a chapel program emphasizing foreign missions, I felt God calling and urging me to commit my life to being a cross-cultural missionary. In surrendering to this call, I felt a tremendous surge of peace and joy. I knew that my commitment pleased the Lord.

During my last year at the seminary, I met Gloria Ann Reece. Gloria is a brown-eyed daughter of Tennessee with brown hair and a ready smile. Her vivacious personality and appearance quickly attracted me. After learning that she was a foreign mission volunteer, I made it a priority to date her. After a year of dating we were married in Brownsville, Tennessee.

In May 1966 Gloria and I both graduated from Southwestern. She received her Master of Religious Education and I received a Bachelor of Divinity (later upgraded to a Master of Divinity).

While we were serving as pastor and wife of Beacon Baptist Church in Shelbyville, Indiana, we began to seek appointment as missionaries with the Foreign Mission Board of the Southern Baptist Convention (now it is the International Mission Board of the SBC).

During that time a momentous event happened to slow down our process. On 5 January 1968, our first child,

Joseph Reece Turman was born! I put up a sign in the window of our small apartment, "It's a boy!" The neighborhood rejoiced with us.

In October 1968, Gloria and I were appointed as missionaries to South Vietnam. In January 1969, we began our missionary orientation at Ridgecrest, North Carolina. Just a few days after the start of orientation, Anne-Marie was delivered at a hospital in Ashville. Now, we would be going to Vietnam with two small children.

Needless to say both of our parents were concerned about us going to Vietnam. The carnage taking place daily there was shown each evening on TV. We tried to assure them that we would not be on the front line of battle.

After missionary orientation we made final packing preparations. We were ready to get on with the going.

Getting On With the Going

The year was 1969. Five hundred and fifty thousand American troops were in Vietnam. The war news was grim. The numbers killed and wounded mounted day by day. The anti-war sentiment rose and became more vocal on campuses throughout America. The day was May 30 and we were leaving for Vietnam on our first missionary journey.

Gloria's family came to say goodbye at the Memphis International Airport. We had just spent several days in Texas saying goodbye to my family.

The farewell was not easy, as they thought of the possibility of never seeing us again. They could not quite believe that we were really going to Vietnam. And now came the difficult time of saying goodbye, the first among many goodbyes at airports.

The boarding call came, and we were off for our exciting missionary adventures...at least, I thought we were off! With eighteen month old Joey in hand, I headed out on the tarmac toward the airplane as Gloria, carrying our six month old daughter, Anne-Marie, spent her last moments with her family. Looking back over my shoulder waving, and urging Joey to wave, I suddenly came to some boarding stairs that were formerly used by airlines for boarding from the tarmac. I led Joey up to the top of these stairs only to discover that there was no airplane for us to enter!

Gloria's mother happened to see this missionary misadventure and exclaimed, "I don't think you all will ever make it to Vietnam!" We did, but not without some bumps along the way.

On June 3, our scheduled flight from Hong Kong to Saigon was cancelled, and we had to take an earlier flight.

We sent a telegram to the Vietnam Baptist Mission office informing them of our new arrival time.

Arriving shortly after 8.00am, we saw a crowd of men in military green fatigues that were there to meet incoming military personnel. We did not see anyone smiling and coming toward us. We soon realized, that in all probability, the telegram that we sent had not arrived. We had pictured being met and welcomed by the mission, and they had planned to do so, but did not know our arrival time.

The Tan Son Nhut airport was crowded with soldiers and a few civilians scattered among them. Vehicles from different units were picking military personnel up in front of the terminal.

You could tell the new arrivals from the veterans. The newbies did not yet have the deep suntan and carried a lot of luggage. They looked around, apprehensively, as blasts of tropical hot air, new sights, sounds and smell, assaulted their senses. The veterans who met them were loud and boisterous, enjoying their roles in initiating Newbies to 'Nam.

Although it was only 9.00am, the morning was already stuffy hot. The airport terminal was only a few degrees cooler than the outside. The floor was dirty, littered with trash and dirt, after having the night and early morning crowds. The sweepers were just arriving to begin their day's work. The heat made us thirsty, but there was nothing for us to drink.

As the crowd dispersed from the terminal, we faced the reality of being in a strange country, without knowing where to go, or what to do. The only ones left in the terminal were a few people sweeping the floor and several taxi drivers.

One of the taxi drivers, who spoke limited English, recognized in us an opportunity for a good fare. He followed us about the airport staying closer than a brother. Since the children were hungry and thirsty and getting to the yelling stage, I knew I had to do something quickly. The situation was deteriorating, and Gloria was beginning to look toward me with a concerned look (now, we know why the International Mission Board issues one-way tickets to first term missionaries).

Finding an old torn and tattered phone book, I thumbed through it until I came to Hoi Truyen Giao Baptit. That seemed to be the nearest thing to a Baptist that I could find, so I called the number. A Vietnamese woman answered the phone, and since I didn't understand anything she said, I hung up. Not having any other number, I tried several more times, but with the same results.

Finally, it came to me that the taxi driver who knew some English could be helpful, so I asked him to speak with the Vietnamese voice at the number I had been calling. He did and was able to get Bob Davis, one of our missionaries, to the phone. Was I ever glad to hear an American voice!

Bob wanted to come and get us, but I told him that we would come by taxi. His coming to pick us up would mean a longer wait at the airport. We were tired, thirsty and ready to go. After Bob told the taxi driver how to get to the Mission office, we crowded into the small taxi with our entire luggage, and merged into the Saigon traffic for an unforgettable first time experience.

The traffic was more like a boiling caldron rather than a flowing current, as dozens of taxis vied for advantage with blaring horns, darting in and out, right and left, contesting military jeeps and trucks. Dozens of motorcycles slipped in between and around vehicles glorying in their maneuverability. To add to this strange mix, that left us dazed and numb, were students on bicycles, and cyclos pedaled by fearless drivers wearing conical shaped straw hats.

The taxi delivered us to the front of the Baptist Mission office. The missionaries royally welcomed us. The disappointment of not being met at the airport was quickly dissolved by the warm welcome. We were taken to the nearby home of Jim and Margaret Gayle. There, along with their gracious hospitality, they served us a large Texas glass of sweet ice tea.

Delightful Days in Dalat

After several days in Saigon, we arrived in Dalat to begin our study of the Vietnamese language. We were ready to begin! After being in the country for more than a week, we realized how helpless and dependent we were on others to help us. It was like being a baby in some ways. Unable to communicate, we had to be led around by others who knew the language and culture.

Dalat is located in the Central Highlands, 120 miles north of Saigon. The cool climate offers a relief from the hot, humid climate of Saigon, or the warm Central Coastal cities. Fresh vegetables, delicious fruits and beautiful flowers are available the year round. Restaurants and hotels are scattered throughout the city to accommodate the year round tourist trade. Dalat was an ideal place to study the language and to adjust to a new culture. As we look back on our missionary career, some of our most delightful days were spent in Dalat.

After staying with David and Barbara Wigger for a week, we moved into an old two-story French style house with green shutters and a cemented yard.

The first night in our house was traumatic. About two o'clock in the morning we were awakened by automatic weapons fire in our back-yard area. We rushed into Joey and Anne-Marie's room, grabbed them up, and lay down on the floor. I could see tracers going by the bedroom window. The gunfire lasted only a few minutes and quit as suddenly as it started.

We were unsure about what had happened. A policeman from the National Police station, located just up the hill from our house, explained that several Viet Cong in the area had a firefight with the police.

21

While studying the language in Dalat, we often heard gunfire and explosions, we but were unable to understand the situations.

Our language study time in Dalat was a happy experience. Our teacher came to our house and taught us while our Vietnamese helper kept our children. Mr. Ngoc loved teaching and took pride in his language. He gave us assignments and expected us to be ready when he came the next day. We studied six to eight hours a day, Monday through Friday, and enjoyed learning a new language. After eighteen months, we finished our formal language training. We had a grasp of the basics, and would spend the next years building on the foundation we received in Dalat.

An Attack on Dalat

While we were studying in Dalat we heard the sounds of war every day. Sometimes, the explosions would be near. One day we heard a particularly loud explosion that jarred our house. We found out later that the Mayor's office had been blown up. On another day, a movie theater was the target.

When we heard these explosions, we would look at our Vietnamese teacher expecting him to react in some way. He never gave the slightest indication that he heard anything. He went on with his teaching without missing a word.

The Vietnamese civilian population, as well as foreigners who had been in Vietnam for a long period of time, focused on the daily demands of life rather than on the war. Once when I was teaching English to students in a house on our street, there was the prolonged sound of gunfire and an explosion. The students never looked up from their studies, or gave any indication that they heard anything.

The next morning, after this shooting activity behind our house, I asked Sam Longbottom, a fellow missionary, if he had heard any shooting and explosions in our neighborhood. He said that he had heard nothing and had slept peacefully all night. I was hesitant to mention anything about the activities of war to our veteran missionaries.

I found that the missionaries, who had experienced a number of years of living under the tensions of war, including the Tet Offensive, didn't want to talk about it. When we gathered as missionaries, we played board games, talked about last furloughs, told funny stories on one another and generally kept the conversation light.

At this time of the war, the Viet Cong and North Vietnamese forces were using Cambodia as a sanctuary.

They would cross the border, launch an attack and run back across the border. The South Vietnamese and US troops were forbidden, at that time, to pursue them across the border.

For this reason, the cities in the Highlands of Central South Vietnam were subjected to terrorist activities such as blowing up public facilities and assassinating South Vietnamese public officials and Army officers.

On a Friday evening, May 1970, we hosted a dinner party for several missionary friends and an US Army sergeant. The dinner party was a success as everyone seem to have a great time.

We had such a good time that we failed to notice that it was 9.50pm. The curfew was at 10.00pm. Our missionary guests rushed out the door saying their farewells on the way to their cars.

Sergeant Will Kurkendyle was stationed at Kraus Compound, which was located across the city. I had promised Will that I would take him back to his base that evening; however, I knew that we didn't have time to beat the curfew.

I apologized to Will for keeping him so late. I told him there was no way for us to beat the curfew. Will said that he could spend the night and return early the next morning.

Will was concerned about the security in our part of town. I told him, "No problem, Will. It's been quiet here."

Our French-built house had an upstairs for the family bedrooms. We had a sleeper downstairs for guests.

Around 2.00am a series of loud explosions and the staccato chatter of automatic weapons jarred Gloria and me awake. The volume of war increased as exploding mortar shells on the National Police Station, two hundred yards up the hill from our house, rattled our windows. The US

Firebase Colgan chimed in with artillery shells whining over our house on their way to targets north of us. I peeked out the window and saw tracers whizzing by from small weapons fire.

Looking out the window toward the part of town where the South Vietnamese Military Academy was located, I could see flares lighting up the entire area. The fierce sounds of war were reverberating across the hills from that direction. It was like the Battle of the Bulge.

I went downstairs to check on Will. He was sitting to the side of a window cradling his M-16. I made a feeble attempt to be humorous, "Like I said, Will, it's secure in this part of town."

He just looked at me without smiling. I could see that he was worried. I was too. Turning, I went back upstairs.

When the mortars began to hit the police station again, Gloria and I took Joey and Anne-Marie downstairs and got under the staircase. I figured that if the VC overshot the police station, they would hit our house. We went up and down the stairs many times that night.

In the early morning hours, we fell into our bed exhausted and went sound asleep.

At daybreak, I was startled out of my deep sleep by the sound of boots pounding on the pavement of the street. Looking out the window, I saw a platoon of South Vietnamese soldiers running with their weapons at port arms. They were heading for an orphanage which was located about five hundred yards up the hill from our house. The VC had taken over the orphanage, which was used as a stronghold during the night of fighting.

Within a short time, the South Vietnamese set up their position, and the battle was on. A helicopter gunship positioned itself just over our house and fired rockets at the VC

25

in the orphanage area. The exploding rockets shook our house with a deafening sound. Will and I stood out in front of the house so we could see some of the action.

Later on, in the middle of the morning, we visited our neighbor next door who worked for USAID. He had a radio and was monitoring the action in the city. He said that fighting was still going on in the middle of the city near the lake. The military academy had been attacked and repulsed with a loss of thirty VC.

Around 3.00pm, a jeep from Will's compound came and picked him up. The soldiers offered to take us to the compound for the night, but we politely declined.

The American soldiers were very helpful and kind to us as missionaries. If we needed anything they would get it for us. At this time, we felt that we would be safer living in our neighborhood than staying on an army base.

We were somewhat apprehensive about the approaching night and what it might bring. Our next-door neighbor stuck his head out, late that afternoon, and warned us not to be shooting at anyone. He said that any kind of hostile action would draw enemy fire. I told him not to worry. We were not going to be shooting at anyone.

Around midnight loud gunfire and explosions were coming from the orphanage area. It lasted about forty minutes, and then everything quieted down for the remainder of the night. The next morning we found out that the VC who were holed up in and around the orphanage had escaped. Around noon we could see people moving about in a normal way.

Many of our missionary friends lived in the Christian and Missionary Alliance Compound out on the edge of Dalat. We were concerned about how they fared during the attack on the city. We decided to drive out and check on them. We, also, wanted to get out of our house and neighborhood for a change, because we had been cooped up for most of the weekend.

Driving up to the CMA compound, we were surprised to see the missionaries all running out to greet us.

They were all obviously excited, asking us, "Why are you here? Isn't the city still under attack?"

They had been cut off from all communication with the outside world, with the exception of listening to the Voice of Australia. The Voice of Australia had reported that Dalat had fallen to the Communist forces. The missionaries were just waiting in the compound, expecting Communist forces to come at any time and capture them. Thus, when we arrived we were given a tumultuous welcome.

It gave us a good feeling to be the bearers of good news that Dalat was secure and back to normal.

Moving from the
Mountain to the Valley

After finishing language study, we moved to Nha Trang. The large, sprawling resort city with wide sandy beaches and palm trees was located on the coast of Central South Vietnam. Nha Trang had US Army, Navy and Green Beret bases. There were, also, bases for the Korean and South Vietnamese forces. Besides all the bases, it had an in-country R&R center for American troops. The city was filled with South Vietnamese, Korean, and American soldiers.

I went down to Nha Trang, alone, to look for a house. Since there were many Americans working there for the US government, and companies under contract with the government, I had difficulty finding a suitable house. The houses suited for western families were already rented out.

Finally, I talked to a Wycliffe Bible translator, and he told me about one of their families who was going on furlough in a few days. They were not renting the house when they came back. I went to look at the house, even though the missionary living there at that time, was out of town.

I noticed that their automobile was chained to the house. That should have told me something about the neighborhood. We later learned that household goods, or anything else not secured, would be stolen. As it seemed to be the only house available at the time, I made arrangements to rent it. The contract would become effective upon the departure of the family living in it.

Moving is a traumatic time for any family at any time. In third world countries, it is even more so. We hired a large truck to take most of our household goods to Nha Trang. I followed the truck in our VW van, which was loaded down with clothes, personal and household items that were more valuable. Gloria and the children would fly down later.

Moving to Nha Trang proved to be a difficult time. The VW van broke down about ten miles from Cam Ranh Bay. The truck was far ahead and continued on without knowing my plight. Aside from being stranded, I had a severe stomach virus. Sitting under a coconut tree I felt washed out and deserted.

Looking up into the sky and seeing the lazy clouds, I remembered the days of being on the farm as a boy. I prayed, "Lord, I've come a long way from Noonday, Texas and here I am sitting in the middle of nowhere. Somehow, I know that You want us here. Now, I'm in real trouble. Help me!"

Through the years, I've found out that when I spread problems or obstacles out before Lord, He often impresses me to take a practical line of action.

This time came the impression that I should get up and flag a ride into Cam Ranh. Jim and Margaret Gayle, fellow Baptist missionaries, lived there with their three boys, Kyle, Kurt and Kent. I did just that. A Vietnamese man gave me a ride to the front of Jim and Margaret's house. He even knew exactly where they lived.

I had some apprehension about leaving our van loaded down with goods, but I had taken our dog, Wolf, with me. Wolf stayed in the van while I caught a ride into Cam Ranh. He proved to be an excellent guard as nothing was missing when I came back with Jim.

Jim graciously responded to my crisis. He took me back to my van and towed it to Cam Ranh. He generously loaned me his van and put my VW van in the garage to be repaired.

I drove on to Nha Trang as I knew the truck would be waiting at our newly rented house. Our household goods were in large crates that had come from the States. The truck driver and I unloaded them in the front yard. We placed strong boards at an angle from the back of the truck to the ground and slid the crates down on these boards.

I felt extremely tired and thirsty. I had nothing to drink, but I knew that I couldn't leave our household goods in the front yard. Even though the house had a fence around it, thieves could enter if they wanted to. The house had running water, but I dared not drink from the faucet. There was a telephone and some telephone numbers scribbled on a piece of paper with the names of several Wycliff missionaries. I called one of the families and explained my predicament to them. They immediately responded by bringing over a large container of water and some food. I drank the entire large container of water. I was on the verge of being dehydrated.

That night, I left Wolf out in the yard and slept on a blanket on the floor in the living room. The next morning, I was up at the crack of dawn. I began to unload the crates, in order to get the house set up with the essentials. Moving many times taught us to set up beds and arrange the kitchen first.

Gloria and the children were to arrive on an Air Vietnam flight at 12:30 p.m. I wanted to get some things ready for their arrival. I went down the street and bought a bottle of coke and drank it warm, as there was no ice. It gave me a burst of energy. I met Gloria, Joey and Anne-Marie on time and brought them to our new house.

It was Gloria's first time to see it. She enthused, "I really like the kitchen and patio arrangement."

After lunch at a small restaurant, we enthusiastically began arranging the furniture in our house. It was a good time, being together again, and setting up our new home.

Getting Started is Just Doing It

The following Saturday, several people from the Phuoc Hai Baptist Church came by to see us. They told us that the previous pastor had moved to Saigon, and that I must preach the next day. I told them that I had just finished language school and was not ready to preach in the Vietnamese language. They stood up, excused themselves, and informed me that I was to preach since there was no one else.

The rest of Saturday was spent in frenzied preparation trying to get ready to bring my first sermon in the Vietnamese language.

After I finished my presentation on Sunday morning, there were some moments of silence. One of the church members, Mrs. Chau, stood up and said, "Missionary, why can't you preach like Missionary Jim Gayle and Missionary Walter Routh? We can't understand what you're trying to say."

I was shocked! After all, I had told them that I was just out of language study and did not want to preach so soon. I had tried my best. Now, why this scathing criticism? And done so publicly. I felt a surge of resentment, but managed to say, "Please pray for me."

The next week, I studied, as much as possible, trying to get ready to face the congregation with a message in the Vietnamese language. After my sermon, Mrs. Chau stood up with the same criticism saying, "Why can't you preach like the other missionaries?" I wanted to say to her, "The missionaries you've mentioned have been here for five and six years and I've just arrived. How do you expect me to preach like them?" However, I just mumbled, "Please pray for me."

The following week I again spent hours getting ready to preach. Mrs. Chau did more for my Vietnamese language than anyone else. Every day I visualized having to face her on Sunday morning, and it drove me to study harder. The third Sunday that I preached, Mrs. Chau did not stand up!

One day, while Gloria was getting the kitchen set up, I was studying the Book of Acts in my office. Reading the Book of Acts excited me, and at that particular time, it spoke to me. Charging into the kitchen, I told Gloria, "I've got to get started, get my feet wet and get things moving for our church in this city!"

She looked up calmly from a bending position, "O.K. just get out there and do it! Just do it!" "Just do it" was not original to Nike.

With that challenge I took my Vietnamese Bible in hand and went to the streets. It was the middle of the afternoon. Walking down the street, I was praying. "Lord, lead me to someone to share with." Going into a bookstore I looked around for a prospect. Not sensing any leadership to share with anyone there, I went on to the Phuoc Hai neighborhood where we had a small Baptist church. Going down one of the streets, I passed a barbershop. The doors were open to the streets. The shop had five chairs, and a number of people were around the shop. I felt this was the place to share the Gospel.

I asked one of the barbers if I could share the *Tin Lanh* (Good News). He gave me permission. Having prepared a five minute sermon from John 3:16, I opened my Bible and launched out on the text that has enough Gospel in it to save the whole world.

While I was preaching, a crowd of about twenty people gathered around the door of the barbershop. When I finished my short message, I thanked the barbers for allowing me to share, and started to leave.

Just then, one of the barbers asked me if I could talk to him in back of the shop. Following him, he led me to a small private room. Then, turning to me he said earnestly, "The Good News that you just spoke about - I've always wanted to know more about it. Can you help me understand it?"

The Holy Spirit was leading in those moments. He took my faltering words and used them to knock at the heart's door of this young Vietnamese barber. He prayed such a heartfelt prayer asking Jesus to come into his life.

Two weeks later, I baptized him in the South China Sea, and he became a member of the Phouc Hai Baptist Church. This experience gave me new confidence in the power of the Gospel of Jesus Christ.

Dead Dogs Don't Lie

Living at 6 Le Dai Hanh street in Nha Trang was, at times, difficult. It was the only suitable house available for us to rent during our first years in Nha Trang. We did rent another house on a much quieter street during our last seven months in the city of Nha Trang.

The first few months gave us a preview of how things were in our neighborhood. Across the street from our house, sitting catty-corner, was a large ramshackle house, where at least fifteen people lived. They worked in the auto body shop business.

Their working place was the street directly beside our front fence.

Promptly at 7:00am, the workers would start banging on auto body parts. This constant banging during the day almost drove us crazy.

I asked them to move to another location. They just looked at me, smiled, and kept on hammering. In desperation, to alleviate the noise, I bought rolls of barbed wire and stretched the wire out some three feet in front of our fence. The wire caused the workers to move their shop across the street from our fence; however, the noise was not diminished very much.

One day, I could see the body shop workers hammering on large tin metal sheets. Curiously, I asked them what they were making from the tin metal sheets. To my astonishment, they said they were going to make a body for a bus.

The volume of noise increased tremendously with the banging on the tin metal sheets. Some days the noise was so bad that we left the house in order to maintain our sanity. Every few weeks I would go out and desperately search for another house to rent. My search was futile.

All the banging and hammering paid off for the auto body shop workers as a bus body began to take shape. The day came when it was finished completely, to our relief. They painted the bus body. The beautifully painted bus body was ready to go, except for a windshield.

We drove a large Ford van that we bought from an American construction company who left Vietnam. The van had a large windshield.

Getting up early each morning, I habitually walked around the house looking at the flowers and checking out the yard. One morning, on my daily stroll around the yard, I passed our Ford van. I noticed that the windshield looked unusually clean. Taking a few steps past the van, I realized that something about this picture was not right!

Wheeling around, I stuck my hand through the opening that held the windshield. My hand confirmed what I saw with my eyes. The windshield was missing!

I charged across the street to look at the bus. It still had no windshield. Four days later, a windshield suddenly appeared in the bus. It looked like the one that came from our Ford van, but there was no way to prove it. Going to the police would have been a futile effort.

Since I had already ordered a windshield from Saigon, I didn't make a case out of it. Once something was stolen from you, kiss it goodbye and get over it. You would never get it back, and no one would be prosecuted.

We had made an effort to become acquainted with our neighbors. Several evenings I had visited the auto body shop workers. One evening I gave them Gospels of John in the Vietnamese language and shared the Good News with them. Several times, Gloria gave them food and clothes. Despite these efforts to befriend our neighbors, dead animals were often thrown into our yard. I would

35

take them out to a deserted beach area and bury them. Burying the dead animals took time away from more constructive activities.

Celebrating our first Christmas in Nha Trang, we arose early to share our gifts. The children had received a generous number of toys from our families in the States. Since we used the Army Post Office (APO) on the nearby military base, all the toys had arrived on time. Among the toys was a tricycle that came in a large box.

After our time of gift sharing, I took the boxes out behind the house.

On the way, I saw a dead dog that had been thrown over the fence into our yard. I knew that I would have to bury the dog soon, or he would begin to stink. Burying the dog on the beach would take time away from the family on Christmas day. Thinking about the dead dog problem, I glanced at the large box that the tricycle had come in. I can put the dog in this box, I thought, and take him out to the beach and bury him in it.

Just then, I had an idea. Why not give the dog a Christmas burial?

I placed the dog in the box and taped the top tightly shut. Plenty of Christmas wrapping paper was left over from the gifts.

Going back into the house, I asked Gloria to wrap the box. She looked at me in amazement when I explained what was in the box. She agreed to wrap the box and turned it into a lovely gift.

I took the beautifully wrapped box and headed for the van. Well, I would have to open the gate first. I placed the box on one of the large cement gateposts and opened the gate. Getting into the van, I backed out of the yard. Getting out of the van, I closed the gate, and got back into the van.

Driving around the block, I knew that I had left the gift-box on the cement gatepost. I went back to see what happened to it. Was the gift-box still on the gatepost? If so, I would bury it on the beach.

Driving back to our gate, I noticed that the gift was gone. I asked Gloria about it. She said that twenty seconds, or so, after I pulled away in the van, a man on a motorcycle roared up, jumped off his cycle, grabbed the gift, jumped back on his motorcycle, and sped away.

Smiling broadly, I said, "Foiled again, Gloria! Now, someone else will have the privilege of giving the dog a Christmas burial."

Sometimes I wish, yes, just wish, I could have seen the face of the man when he opened the beautifully wrapped gift. Dead dogs don't lie!

Getting Out the Gospel in Nha Trang

As the Vietnamese Pastor of the Phuoc Hai Church had just left, and most of the able bodied men and women members of the church worked long hours, there was no one to work with me in evangelism. I went witnessing alone and it was difficult. I needed a counterpart to work with me in evangelism. Gloria and I begin to pray for someone to go with me.

One day, as we were resting at the noon hour, someone banged on our front gate. We had a fence around our house with a gate that was kept locked much of the time.

Usually, no one visited at this hour. It was a time when people had a light lunch and rested from the heat of the day. Curious, I went out to see who would come at that hour. A young man in the uniform of the South Vietnamese Air Force stood there. Speaking to him without opening the gate, I asked him what he wanted.

He countered with a question, "Are you the Baptist Missionary who goes out witnessing?" After I replied in the affirmative, he said, "Can I go with you? I've just been transferred here. I'm Long Pham and a member of the Grace Baptist Church in Saigon."

Opening the gate and leading him in to the house, I called to Gloria who was looking from a window, "Praise the Lord! Our prayer has been answered!"

Our prayer was, indeed, answered in Long Pham's coming. When he had a day off, we would go out together visiting prospects and sharing the Gospel.

Long Pham, being a believer for several years, was grounded in the Gospel. Since we had seminary extension courses available, I begin to teach him several courses. In his work as an air controller with the South Vietnamese Air force he had some free time at the airport. He used this time to study the extension courses. A course on preaching was one of the courses he was studying. I invited him to rotate with me on Sundays in preaching.

One day, while we were out witnessing, Long Pham suggested that he and I get up at four-thirty, five mornings a week, to pray at the church. He mentioned that the Buddhist Monks were up before that time every morning. With that challenge I agreed to his suggestion. The first few mornings I had to force my body out of bed. Then, I started on a routine of drinking four or five glasses of water after getting out of bed, followed by a cup of black coffee. This activated my groggy body and prepared me for the coming day.

Long Pham and I asked the Lord for ten new families for our congregation. We shared this vision with our church people and they begin to pray, witness and visit. This was in January, and by December, we had more than ten new families added to our congregation.

God does answer prayer! During that year we put a lot of feet to our prayers. Our church became involved in sharing with their families and friends.

At the end of the year we had a large group of young people. The Christmas of 1973, Gloria organized the first Christmas drama for the church. The children and young people enthusiastically took part in it. The members of the church were so pleased that they had put on their first Christmas drama.

Gloria had a vibrant ministry with our children, as well as with the women in the church. One day, two children in Gloria's class, Hoa and Phuong, came to our house, and asked Gloria to come and pray for their mother, Ba Bich, who was seriously ill. Gloria prayed for this sick mother, and, also, helped out with some much needed food for the household. Shortly after Gloria's visit, Ba Bich improved and soon recovered fully from her sickness.

Ba Bich's husband had left for the army, and she had not heard from him in two years. Like so many women in South Vietnam, whose husbands left and never came back, they were left destitute and had to take any job they could get to feed the family. Ba Bich had lost her previous job and had not worked for some time. Her relatives gave them just enough food to stay alive.

During one of Gloria's visits with Ba Bich, she led her to know Christ, as Savior and Lord. Ba Bich became a fervent follower of Christ.

Gloria taught her about the privilege of prayer and encouraged her to bring her needs to the Lord. Ba Bich began to ask the Lord for a job. One afternoon, she came knocking at our gate, excitedly telling Gloria, even before she was in the yard, that the Lord had given her a job. A man had come looking for her to work with the street sweepers. This was a miracle in itself, as so many people wanted jobs and, usually, a foreman never went looking for people. Ba Bich was a great blessing to our church as she became a dynamic witness and prayer warrior.

Living in a centrally located city like Nha Trang, we often had missionary and Vietnamese guests to spend the night. One week we had an unusual number of our missionary friends to come by. Since we, as a Mission, were family, our Missionary Kids (MKs) called other missionaries "Aunt" and "Uncle." That particular week, our children, Joey and Anne-Marie, became better acquainted with Uncle Jim Humphries, Uncle Jim Gayle, Uncle Bob Davis, Uncle Peyton Moore and Uncle Sam Longbottom. One day at lunch, the day after the visits of all these "uncles" to our home, I asked Anne-Marie, our three year old, to pray.

There was a long pause as she formed in her mind the words she would use in her prayer. Now, she had it. It was so natural and so family: "Dear Uncle Jesus".

Sometimes our missionary friends would only have time to drop by for a cold drink and use the bathroom. Often we had problems with our commodes. On one occasion our commode would not flush, so we had a bucket sitting under the faucet to flush the commode. To make sure that our guests would know the correct procedure, I put a sign over the faucet that read: "Please use the bucket." Our first missionary friend that dropped by that week did use the bucket!

Going into Judea with the Gospel

While we were out on one of our witnessing missions, Long Pham said to me, "There's a small island off the coast of Nha Trang that has around fifteen hundred people, mostly fishermen. I feel strongly that we should go there and try to start a church."

I agreed with him, "We need to always be reaching out. How about us going to the island next Tuesday when you're off duty?"

The following week, we rented a fishing boat and headed for the island. Landing on the island, we were welcomed in a way that we did not expect. About a dozen children between the ages of ten and fourteen picked up rocks on the shore and began throwing the rocks at us. We begin to run and dodge the rocks and sought protection behind some coconut trees in the yard of a small house. The owner of the house, seeing our predicament, came out and chased the children away. He then invited us into his house.

After serving us hot tea, we had the opportunity to get to know one another. He asked us who we were and why we had come to the island. We told him that we were Good News people and had come to share the Gospel of Christ.

Immediately interested, he asked, "I've heard something of the Gospel of Jesus Christ, but I've never been clear about it. Can you help me understand it?"

For the next hour Long and I had the joy of sharing the Good News with Mr. Tuan. Then the three of us knelt as Mr. Tuan opened his heart to the risen Lord Jesus. Two months later, we baptized Mr. Tuan and started a Bible study in his home.

The church on the island grew with new believers as time went by. Being one of the few tailors on the island, Mr.

Tuan knew many people. He used his trade, as a tailor, to witness.

Coming back from the island one day, on a crowded taxi boat, an opportunity to start a new Bible study was presented to Long Pham and me. While on the boat, we met some fishermen who lived on the mainland coast in a village just over the mountain from the village of Cau Da. They wanted us to come and start a Bible study in their village. They said we would need to get permission from the village leader.

Cau Da is located on the south coast of Nha Trang seven kilometers from the center of the city. It is a bustling little town that has an excellent fish market. It serves as a harbor for the fishing boats, tourist boats and commercial ships.

We agreed to come the following Tuesday morning. At the appointed time, we came to Cau Da, parked the car, and began to walk over the mountain to the fishing village. It was only about two kilometers to the village, but over very rough and mountainous terrain. About half-way, there was a village on the summit of this small mountain.

Something very strange happened as we entered this village and began to walk through it to get to our destination. A chorus of high-pitched voices was raised in an eerie and continuous sound that grew louder and more irritating as we progressed into the village. It seemed as if the entire village was participating.

Long Pham stopped and said to me, "These people are demon possessed. The demons are crying out through them." Then, Long Pham shouted out, *"Ta nhon danh Jesus Christ: Em lang!"* "I command you in the name of Jesus Christ: Be quiet!"

At that very moment, it was as if a faucet was turned off. Everything became deathly quiet. I could hear the sound of our footsteps as we walked out of the village.

43

When we arrived in the village of the fishermen, we were greeted warmly. We met in the house of the village leader. He was an older man with a white goatee who resembled Ho Chi Minh. Twenty-five people crowded into his humble, but spacious front room. Straw mats were provided for all as we sat on the dirt floor. After we were served tea and fish chips, we began to share with the leader how we would like to start a Bible study in his village.

Just as the leader was responding to us, we were interrupted by a woman who had suddenly entered the house. She was very excited and was waving toward the leader. He motioned for her to come to where he was sitting on the mat. She politely sat and scooted on the mat to him. Then she excitedly whispered to the leader while gesturing with both hands.

As Long Pham was sitting next to the leader, he leaned forward to hear what the woman was saying. Hearing all that he needed to hear, Long turned to me and said, "This woman says that a group of men are waiting to ambush us on the way back to Cau Da."

The village leader, looking at both Long and me, said, "You must leave quickly! You will not be safe here. One of the fishermen will take you out by boat."

A fisherman, who was sitting with us in the house, stood up and volunteered his boat. The village was located in a beautiful little cove. The fishing boats were anchored out in the bay about fifty yards from the shore. Long Pham and I began to prepare to swim to the boat. The fisherman gestured wildly saying, "No, no, you get in the basket and I'll swim push you to the boat!"

The "basket" was a large round straw basket measuring four feet in diameter and coated with a fish brine like glue that made it water proof. The fishermen used it to go back and forth to the shore from their anchored boats.

Thinking that I might be too large for the basket, I protested, "I'm too large to get in this basket. I'll swim!"

The fisherman had no time for such talk. Pointing at the basket, he said firmly, "You get in now! We must go!"

I crawled into the basket with Long Pham and away we went to the boat. I was surprised at how smooth the ride was in the basket. The fisherman took us out of the cove and on to Cau Da where the car was parked. We never did have an opportunity to return to that village. Security was getting to be a problem in the area, and we were advised not to go there again.

In January 1999, Gloria and I returned to Vietnam with our son, Joey, and our daughter-in-law, Stephanie, and our granddaughter, Kaitlin.

Returning to Nha Trang, Joey and I rented a boat and returned to the island to see if Mr. Tuan was still alive and the church was still going on. An entourage joined us as we headed for Tuan's house. One of the people in the group knocked on his door. When he came to the door, they asked him, "Do you know this man?" Without changing expression Tuan answered, "Yes, he's the missionary."

Entering his house I saw the Bible that I had given to him some thirty years ago. A large cross on the wall testified that he was a follower of Christ.

After some minutes of conversation, I asked Tuan how many believers were on the island. He glanced at the crowd of people looking in the door and windows, and leaned over and whispered to me, "I can't say much here, but there are very many."

A Vision Becomes A Reality

Another day as Long and I were on the boat heading over to the island, he suddenly declared, "Someday, I'm going to be a missionary just like you."

I wanted to encourage him, yet I was thinking that he, probably, would never get out of South Vietnam. The war was not going well for the South. Thinking these thoughts, I responded, "Wonderful! Praise the Lord! Maybe you can go to Laos or Cambodia."

Long disagreed, "No, I'm going to other countries just like you."

Not wanting to discourage him, I supported him by saying, "That's tremendous Long. May God be with you."

While saying this, I felt a touch of sadness for I was thinking that, in all probability, Long Pham would never leave South Vietnam.

In August 1974 Long was transferred back to Saigon to work as an air controller at Tan Son Nhut Air Base. During the two years he served in Nha Trang, our church had grown numerically and spiritually. At that time, Gloria and I could not understand why the Lord allowed Long Pham to be taken away from such a fruitful ministry.

During the tumultuous last days in Saigon, Long Pham, with the help of missionary Walter Routh, was able to use his place and position at Tan Son Nhut to get 48 Baptists, including some of his family and friends, out of Vietnam on one of the last flights. If Long Pham had remained in Nha Trang, he probably would not have escaped out of South Vietnam.

Long Pham was a refugee for several days at Clark Air Base in the Philippines. Our family had left Vietnam before the invading North Vietnamese had taken over Saigon. We had come to Baguio City, Philippines. While Long and the other Vietnamese refugees were at Clark, I had the opportunity of encouraging him and the other refugees while serving as a volunteer translator for the Air Force.

Clark Air Base was the staging area for the refugees as they were moved out to Guam and other places in the world. Long Pham, along with Walter Routh, and hundreds of other refugees, went from Clark Air Base to Guam. From Guam, they went on to Camp Pendleton.

By that time, our family had arrived home for a short furlough, and I was invited by Dr. Keith Parks to go to Camp Pendleton to serve among the refugees. While at Pendleton, I was able to organize church services for Baptists and others who wanted to attend.

A Baptist church in Birmingham, Alabama eventually adopted Long Pham. He enrolled at Samford University, where he graduated with a BA degree. From Samford, Long went on to Southern Baptist Theological Seminary in Louisville, Kentucky. While at the seminary, Long Pham met Mary, the daughter of a Vietnamese pastor. They were married during his time at the seminary.

When we were on furlough in 1984, from Indonesia, I received a telephone call from Long. I could feel the excitement in his voice as he told me that he, and his wife, Mary, were being appointed as Southern Baptist missionaries to the Philippines.

At that moment, in my memory, I could hear him saying, as we were on the boat heading for the island, "I'm going to be a missionary just like you!" Then, I didn't think it was possible. But God knew, and He planted the vision in Long Pham's heart and mind of being an international missionary. That vision became a reality.

God Loves the Little Kittens

In the spring of 1972, the North Vietnamese, attacked the northern provinces of South Vietnam, caused thousands of refugees to flee to the south. Thousands of refugees came pouring into Nha Trang on trucks, buses, taxis, or whatever means of transport they could get on.

Everywhere I went in the city I saw refugees. Most of them were women, children and older men. The collateral fallout of war always seems to impact this segment of society.

They all had the same look on their faces: they were tired, disoriented, fearful and with a hopeless outlook. Most of them had lost all of their material goods, including their houses. Many had lost loved ones.

As I drove about the city looking over the situation, I felt helpless. What can I do? What can we do as a small group of Christians? In my mind, I was thinking, "This is the South Vietnamese government's problem. They have the responsibility to take care of it." In my heart, I didn't feel right about doing nothing.

Returning home, I told Gloria about the situation in the city. She simply asked, "What are we going to do to help them?"

Heading into my office, I replied, "I don't know. What can we do? We are such a small group. We do not have the resources to help anyone."

Sitting at my desk, I tried to concentrate on preparing a Bible study. The picture of a young Vietnamese mother sitting at the city square with her three children kept coming back to my mind. She had an empty stare that showed no recognition of anyone else around her. Her face reflected disillusionment and despair.

I was startled out of my reflection by Gloria's voice outside the door of my office. "You'll have to ask your Dad. If he thinks its O.K., we'll keep him."

Standing in the door, Gloria explained the problem. "Joey and Anne-Marie want to adopt another kitten. He was just outside our fence. I told them that we could, if you give permission."

My office was located in a small building at the back of the house with a patio between it and the house. Going outside my office, I saw Joey and Anne-Marie standing on the patio clutching a ragged, dirty little kitten.

I said to them, "Listen, we've adopted three kittens in the last few weeks. We can't keep taking in every cat that comes up to our fence. Besides, these cats off the streets carry diseases. It's not healthy to take them in. No, we can't adopt any more kittens."

Holding the kitten to her breast, Anne-Marie's lower lip quivered and tears came rolling down both cheeks. Then, she stated her case: "Daddy, God loves the little kittens."

I wasn't expecting God to be brought into the kitten problem. It took me by surprise. But it shouldn't have, for we read Bible stories to our children before they could walk or talk. We emphasized how God made every living creature and that He loves, in a special way, all the children of the world. God also cares for the kittens, puppies and animals of the world.

Confronted with such a theological truth, how could I toss that dirty little kitten back out into a dangerous street? Not only that, how could I tell another Bible story about God's loving concern for all the creatures of the world?

Relenting before the tears of a three year old, and the fact that God does love all the kittens of the world, I said that we could keep the kitten.

Going back to my office I kept thinking about the thousands of refugees. They were thrown out on dangerous streets. If God loves the little kittens, He certainly loves the refugees. If God loves the refugees, then we must love them. If we love the refugees, then we must help them, I thought.

I called our mission office in Saigon. Getting one of our missionaries on the telephone, I asked him about funds for helping the thousands of refugees from the recent war offensive. He said that we had funds that could be used for that purpose, and he would immediately send them to us.

In the meantime, Gloria and I thought we would do something for the refugees. We went downtown and bought two hundred loaves of French bread and put them in the back of our van.

Driving out to the middle of the refugee camp, we began to hand out the loaves of bread. Hundreds of hungry refugees mobbed us! The mob pushed and shoved so much that we retreated to our van. Once inside the van, we quickly handed the remaining bread out the car windows.

Later that evening, I told our Vietnamese church members about our experience. They smiled politely and said, "Bread is not what they need, and that's not the way to do it."

We should have consulted with them before we attempted to do anything.

Our Vietnamese leaders suggested that we use the money to buy bags of rice. If the Vietnamese have rice, they reasoned, they can make it. They can add whatever they want to the rice.

"The way to hand out the rice," they said, "is to have the family leaders come and get the rice for their families." The head of the family would present his family papers. The family papers would list the number of family members.

The next morning we went and bought fifty 100- pound bags of rice. We hired a truck to take the bags of rice to our church where the bags were stored in the back of the building. Using our van, we took ten bags at a time to the refugee camp.

Gloria and I were amazed at how well the Vietnamese handled the distribution. The heads of the families lined up in an orderly way. They politely took their rice and took it back to their families. It was so different from the chaos that we had experienced the day before.

We gave out Gospels of John and other Christian literature to those who came for rice. From this experience, Gloria and I learned again the necessity of working together with our national brothers and sisters in carrying out a program.

Oh yes, there was something else that I learned from that experience. God loves the little kittens.

The Fresh Winds of Revival

During the last week in November 1974, we had our annual prayer retreat in Dalat. The insecure condition of the country at that time had made traveling more dangerous. We were thankful when the last missionary family arrived safely. I was the chairman for the Prayer Retreat Committee and responsible for leading the committee to plan and organize the program and other activities for the retreat. The unstable conditions and communication problems resulted in my not getting together with the other missionaries on the committee. When I arrived in Dalat with my family, I immediately met with the other committee members. It was obvious that they were very concerned about the insufficient planning for the retreat. When we met together they were giving me the "well, what are we going to do" looks.

Avery Willis saved the day. Avery, who was a missionary to Indonesia, was invited to lead us in our Bible study and devotional times. He joined us after our committee had met for a few minutes. His first question was, "What's the program?"

One of the members of the committee informed him, "We have no program."

Avery raised both hands and face toward heaven, "Praise the Lord! I've always wanted to be in a meeting where nothing is planned. Let the Holy Spirit lead us!"

From that moment on I knew that we would have an unusual prayer retreat. Our committee did put together some basic operating structure for the retreat, but there was flexibility and freedom for spontaneous participation. During and after the first meeting there was evidence of the movement of the Holy Spirit among us.

Avery's first message pointed out how sin not only severs our fellowship with God but also with one another. He emphasized how our sins need to be forsaken and confessed. Two journeymen, young men who came to serve over a two-year period, stood and confessed their ill feelings toward one another. Their testimonies, both humorous and touching, paved the way for others to share openly.

During the night I could hear people going up and down the hall talking in low, muffled voices. The next morning during breakfast, I heard about a meeting that had taken place around the fireplace and had lasted until 4.00am. There was a sharing of burdens and several had made things right between each other. You could sense that something was taking place that could only be attributed to a movement of the Holy Spirit.

All that day there was a spirit of brokenness among us. Both men and women would rise to share a testimony and begin to weep, unable to finish.

Saturday night, in a sharing time around the fireplace, Prissy Tunnell said that for the past several weeks she had a ringing in her ears that was driving her toward a nervous breakdown. She pleaded for us to pray for her. Immediately, many of us gathered around her and prayed for her healing. She was healed at that moment. The noise in her ears was gone. We all joined her in praising the Lord!

Her healing heightened our awareness that God was doing something new and unusual among us. The next morning a group went out to pray for a Vietnamese pastor who was very ill. He was healed of his sickness.

During that time the Holy Spirit aroused a deep spirit of concern in our hearts for those who had not experienced Christ. Jim and Barbara Lassiter asked Gloria and myself to come to their house in Dalat to witness to their Vietnamese helper, Bich Lin. They were new language students, and were not yet ready to bring a clear witness to their helper in the Vietnamese language. They yearned for her salvation and had been praying for her.

After we shared the plan of salvation with Bich Lin, she was willing to confess her sins and invite Christ into her heart.

However, when we asked her if she possessed eternal life, she would answer, "Someday I shall be saved."

It was obvious that Bich Lin was not clear about the great transaction that takes place when a person repents and trusts in Christ as Lord and Savior. We, patiently, went over the Scriptures with her again.

When we asked her about her salvation, she continued to say, "Someday I will be saved." The thought came to me that I needed to picture for Bich Lin what happens when we repent and turn to Christ seeking His forgiveness. I took a piece of paper and asked her to take it to the kitchen table.

I told her, "Bich Lin, each time you think of a sin that you have committed in the past, make a mark on the paper." After about ten minutes Bich Lin handed me the piece of paper that was covered with pencil marks.

Then, dramatically holding up the paper, I announced to her, "These are your sins! Watch what happens to them when you come to Christ asking His forgiveness." Taking a match I lit the paper and burned it to ashes.

You could see the light of understanding spread over Bich Lin's face. She stood up and begin to pace around the room saying, "I am forgiven! I am forgiven! Jesus has forgiven me of all my sins!"

Then Bich Lin rushed out of the house and went down the street and through the neighborhood telling her friends and neighbors that Jesus had forgiven her.

After the revival retreat, we came down the mountain to Nha Trang to continue our ministry. In the first church service at Phuoc Hai I stood and shared with the believers how God had moved among us. I asked their forgiveness for the times when my attitude and words had not been appropriate toward them and pleasing to God.

Their faces registered the same inscrutable looks as before, but I could tell that they understood and knew that something had happened in our lives.

During that time our church services and evangelism took on a new dimension of power. We became bolder and more urgent in our witness.

Mass Communications, directed by Peyton Moore, had radio programs in Nha Trang that broadcast studies in the Gospel of John. A Bible study on the Gospel of John was sent to those who wrote and requested it. Peyton sent hundreds of names to us, of those who lived in Nha Trang. We formed three teams from our church to follow up on each of the names sent to us. This resulted in a number of new people coming to confess Christ as Savior and coming into our church.

One morning I was pushing my bicycle down the street to a repair shop. Two South Vietnamese soldiers called from across the street asking me to wait on them. They wanted to talk with me. Approaching me, they asked if I was a missionary. After I replied in the affirmative, they asked, "How can we be forgiven of our sins?"

Using a New Testament I guided them to the One who has the power to forgive sin, even Jesus Christ. After praying with them, they continued on their way.

While waiting in the shop for the minor repairs on my bicycle, the shop owner whose office was upstairs sent word that he wanted to talk with me. Wondering what the owner wanted, I went upstairs to meet him.

He did not waste any time in telling me what was on his mind. He said, "I'm a Christian, but I'm backslidden. Can you help me get right with the Lord?"

I turned to 1 John 1:9 and asked him to read the verse aloud. Then, I asked him if he believed the promise given in the verse. After he affirmed that he did, I prayed for him, and then asked him to pray. He prayed a fervent prayer confessing his sins and asking for forgiveness.

Getting off his knees he had a radiant smile on his face. He thanked me for coming. Accompanying me downstairs, he refused to accept pay for the repair of my bicycle.

Riding my bike down the street near our house I met five South Vietnamese soldiers. They greeted me warmly, and then asked me if I was a missionary or pastor. After acknowledging that I was a missionary, they asked me if I could help them find forgiveness for their sins. I gave each one a Gospel of John from the pouch I carried on the bicycle and shared with them how Jesus will forgive the sins of those who come in faith to Him and give them eternal life. All five knelt and prayed with me a prayer of confession of sin and faith in Him who has the power to forgive sin and give life eternal.

The impending crisis looming over South Vietnam resulted in thousands of people thinking about their spiritual destiny. During those last weeks in Nha Trang, we had the opportunity to counsel with dozens of people about their spiritual life.

Earl Bengs, Baptist missionary serving in Dalat, and I had worked together in planning a spiritual retreat for our church pastors and leaders. We held the meeting in our Good News Center in Nha Trang. Walter Routh came from Quang Ngai Province to help lead in the sessions. Ten church leaders came with him to attend the retreat. The

Good News Center was packed out with around sixty men in attendance. These men came from Nha Trang, Cam Ranh, Dalat and Quang Ngai.

Warm fellowship, spirited singing and enthusiasm characterized the retreat. During the late afternoon of the second day, the entire tone of the retreat was changed as we received word that the city of Ban Me Thuoc had suddenly been attacked and captured by the North Vietnamese. The fall of Ban Me Thuot was an unmistakable sign that South Vietnam was in a very critical situation.

The evening service was very somber. Some of the men stood and gave spontaneous testimonies. Even though the Vietnamese are not given to public displays of emotion, many of the men wept openly as they shared how God had moved in their lives. The crisis seemed to open the door to release emotions that had been pent up, perhaps for years. There was confession of sin, a time of praising the Lord while giving thanks for His goodness, and a time for mutual encouragement and support.

During that time the Holy Spirit moved in bringing revival to church pastors and leaders in preparing them for the difficult days ahead.

As Earl Bengs, Walter Routh and I met after the evening service at our house, we felt led to change the theme and direction of the next day's meetings. In the light of the critical situation we felt led to have seminars on the subject of "The Church Living and Serving in Difficult Times of Persecution." It was a very timely theme and the discussions were very lively. It was only to be a short time before these men were actually living under the duress of a new and oppressive government.

The Beginning of the End

In August 1974, a day after President Nixon had resigned as president, Fred Donner and I were eating a hamburger in the American Club at Nha Trang. Fred, a Wycliffe missionary, had graduated from the University of Minnesota as a history major, and was a keen observer of political and military happenings in the world.

Speaking of President Nixon's recent resignation, he predicted: "Joe, get a suitcase packed. We won't be here much longer. The North Vietnamese are coming. They would have come sooner, but they were afraid of Nixon."

Fred was right in his predictions, for the North Vietnamese moved in with force to occupy Phuoc Binh Province, northwest of Saigon, on 9 January 1975. There was no protesting outcry from the US, or any other world power. It was as if the world was tired of Vietnam and wished that it would just go away.

Security was becoming a problem for us. We had to be more careful about our traveling. On one occasion, Jim Kellum, a fellow Baptist missionary, Anh Phat, a schoolteacher, and myself were going to Tuy Hoa, at the invitation of a village leader, to hold evangelistic services.

On Highway One, we joined a South Vietnamese convoy as the last vehicle. Winding through a mountain pass, the first six trucks were hit by a Viet Cong ambush. We waited in our vehicle until the fighting moved away from the convoy to the mountains, and then continued on our way to Tuy Hoa.

While we were holding preaching services in the village near Tuy Hoa, Anh Phat was very nervous and kept looking at his watch. He knew that we had to go back through the same mountains where we were ambushed.

There were reasons for him to be concerned about the time because after 4.00pm it was more insecure out in the rural areas. He knew, also, what the Viet Cong did to South Vietnamese Patriots, if they were captured, especially, those traveling with Americans. They were disemboweled and left lying in a conspicuous place to frighten and intimidate the local population.

We finished the evangelistic services at 2.30pm and sped back through the mountains crossing them by 3.30pm. That was our last trip to Tuy Hoa.

During the last few months in Nha Trang we became acquainted with Linda Thoi and her husband, Captain Thoi. He was an outstanding South Vietnamese officer who had received the best education and training possible in South Vietnam before receiving additional training in America. While he was receiving training at Ft. Sam Houston in San Antonio, Texas, he met Linda, a beautiful Hispanic lady. They fell in love, were married and Linda came to Vietnam with him.

Linda was a devout Christian and a Baptist church member. She found out where the Phouc Hai church was located and begin to attend church. Captain Thoi accompanied her whenever he was free from his duties.

As we became better acquainted with Linda and Captain Thoi, we often invited them over for dinner. One evening after dinner, Captain Thoi and I were having an animated discussion about the war and politics. He suddenly asked me if I had a map of Vietnam. I fetched the map from my office and spread it out on a small table in the living room. He showed me the places where he projected the North Vietnamese would attack very shortly.

Then, turning to me, he earnestly advised, "Joe, if I were you, I would get Gloria and the children and leave

59

Vietnam. The North Vietnamese can close down Tan Son Nhut anytime they want to."

After the fall of Saigon, the North Vietnamese corroborated Captain Thoi's statement saying that they did not close Tan Son Nhut because of the presence of many American civilians. The closure of Tan Son Nhut would have made it necessary for the American military to intervene to get out their citizens.

About a week before the fall of Nha Trang thousands of refugees poured into the city from the provinces north of us. They were fleeing before the attacking North Vietnamese Army. Approximately thirty thousand refugees were housed in tents north of the city. Our Good News Center was housing between seventy and eighty Baptist church members from the churches north of us.

From our Phuoc Hai Baptist Church we formed teams of men to help distribute bags of rice to the refugees. The rice was bought with money contributed by the Baptist World Alliance. Our teams, also, handed out thousands of Gospels of John in the Vietnamese language to the refugees.

It was a touching experience, as an American, to walk through the refugee camp. Dozens of Vietnamese approached me weeping, asking if I could help them find a loved one who was lost, or left behind in their hasty flight from the NVA. Many came kneeling and pleading with me to take them with me to America. There were many who asked when the American army was coming to save South Vietnam. These questions made me feel sad, because I knew no help was coming.

The last Sunday that we were in Nha Trang, we were getting ready to walk out the door to attend eight o'clock Sunday School when we heard someone pounding on the gate. Going out, I saw that it was Linda Thoi. Before I could open the gate she called to me that she did not have time to come in. She said that Captain Thoi had sent her to tell us that it was time for us to leave. The North Vietnamese army had broken through a hotly contested pass some thirty to forty miles north of us, and they would soon be in Nha Trang.

Telling Gloria to pack us a light suitcase, I went to the American Consulate. Getting permission to go into his office, I found the Consul sitting behind his desk, disheveled, unshaved and red-eyed. Obviously, he had not slept. Telling him the news that I had heard, he verified that it was true.

He added, "It's a critical situation. We'll start evacuating Americans tomorrow."

That Sunday night Captain Thoi came by in a jeep with two of his men. He requested two bags of rice. After loading the rice he paused, and speaking in a low voice so that his men could not hear, he asked, "Would you leave the keys to your vans here with your helper? We may need them to escape to the coast."

I told him that I would do so. We never saw Captain Thoi again. To this very day we do not know what happened to him and Linda.

As far as the two vans (one was left at my house by Jim Kellum who was on furlough), they were taken by our Baptist orphanage in Cam Ranh (by this time we were in Saigon). Mr. Ha, the director, crammed ninety orphans into our two vans, plus the van he had, and escaped ahead of the NVA to the coast in Phan Rang. There, they bought an old fishing boat and headed out to sea. Several days out at sea they ran out of water and food. Crying out to the Lord they were miraculously rescued and taken to Singapore by a commercial ship.

Monday morning I went to the Consulate expecting to be told that we would be evacuated sometime that day. Instead, I was in for a big surprise. A lady from the Consulate, looking to be in her early forties, was appointed to be over the evacuation of American citizens and their dependents. The Consul was packed full of people. Americans and their Vietnamese wives and children, construction workers, businessmen and others had come out of the woodworks. They all wanted to be evacuated as soon as possible.

Working my way through the crowd, I asked the lady when were we going to be evacuated out. She replied, "There's really no big hurry. We're going to get all the Vietnamese dependents out first, and then we'll get to you."

I could not believe what I heard. My voice expressing the urgency that I felt, "I know how critical this situation is! You have a responsibility to get our wives and children out of here as soon as possible."

The dear lady looked so sad in that moment knowing that what I said was true. She gently said to me, "You come back at one this afternoon. We'll make arrangements for them as soon as possible,"

Coming back at one that afternoon, I found the Consulate still crammed with people. The lady in charge saw me and motioned for me to come. She told me that the wives and children of the missionaries were scheduled to go out at ten o'clock the following morning.

The next morning we were up early to prepare for the flight. Gloria wisely packed the irreplaceable items in the one suitcase, like our family pictures and memos from the years.

The departure of our wives and children for Saigon was a sad time for us men. There were so many uncertainties. Provinces were falling and the entire infrastructure of our city was crumbling with numbing rapidity. The banks were already closed. Most of the police had abandoned their post. Renegade army deserters were roaming the streets, taking what they wanted at gunpoint.

When the Air America DC-3 taxied up for boarding, we men could not but wonder if we would see our wives and children again.

Last Days in Vietnam

Arriving back at our house from the airport, I saw that a group from the Phouc Hai Baptist church was waiting to see me. They wanted to continue the distribution of rice and Scripture portions to the refugees.

Immediately we loaded the van and several boxes of Gospels of John and headed for the refugee camp. The refugees seemed to be grateful for the rice, and, even more so, for the Gospels of John. After we had distributed several boxes of the Gospels, hundreds of refugees were asking if we could bring more. We knew that the Word of Life was more important to them than the temporary rice. Many of these refugees had narrowly escaped death. They were hungry to know more about eternal life.

That evening, and several evenings following, we had worship services at the Good News Center where we had housed sixty plus refugees. The services lasted more than two hours with fervent singing, testimonies and pointed, brief sermons. There was a special bonding of fellowship that happens to those brought providentially together in a crisis.

Our house was located only a half a block from the Good News Center. Leaving the Center after the services, I returned to an empty house. It was then that I missed Gloria and the children. The nights were punctuated by the sounds of gunfire. I wondered and waited, along with the city, to see what the morning would bring upon us.

Early Thursday morning, a delegation from the Baptists in the Cam Ranh area, came to see me. They had heard that thousands of people would be evacuated from the Danang area to Cam Ranh. They wanted to get their social center set up and ready to minister to the thousands of people who would be coming there.

They needed money for rice and other provisions. They asked me if I would go to Saigon and get the money that was needed. They had heard that the Baptist World Alliance had sent money to be used in this time of crisis. I told them that I would go that afternoon, if I could get a flight out.

Before I left for Saigon I wanted to check with our landlord about the rent for the future. The future looked dark for South Vietnam, but I wanted to make sure that we would have our house if, by providence, we could remain to serve in Nha Trang. The landlord owned a hardware shop in downtown Nha Trang. As it was only a short distance, I went by foot.

On the way I met several Vietnamese with whom I had an acquaintance. They begged me to take them with me when I left. I told them that I was going to see my landlord and pay my rent. This seemed to help them get a handle on their emotions.

Arriving at the landlord's shop, I told him that I had come to pay our rent. He wanted a year in advance, but I told him that I wanted to pay three months only. He told me, "There's no need to worry. Our cowboys are going to hold them. They're winning the battles up north of us."

Just when he finished speaking, one of his workers came in from trying to get Air Vietnam tickets to Saigon. He told his boss, "There's none available. They're all sold out!"

The landlord lost his cool. He jumped up and began to pace around his shop mumbling, "What are we going to do? What are we going to do?"

Leaving that question unanswered, I quickly left the shop and made my way back to the house to get ready for my afternoon flight.

I could see that the city was on the verge of complete chaos. Bands of deserting South Vietnamese soldiers roamed the streets carrying their M-16s. The local criminals were beginning to take advantage of the chaos.

Calling our mission office, I talked to our mission treasurer, Sam Longbottom. He said they had the money for the Cam Ranh project. Getting on an Air America flight to Saigon, I arrived about 3:30 p.m. Ken Goad, our mission business manager, met me at the airport.

Driving through the city on our way to the office I was telling Ken that the situation was critical and that we needed to get our wives and children out of the country. Ken just looked at me and said nothing. Looking out the car windows as we drove through the city, I could see people lined up to get into movie theaters. People were going about life as if nothing was happening.

Coming to Saigon was like coming into another world. The tension and chaos of Nha Trang was not yet in Saigon. Actually, Saigon had been cordoned off by some of their best troops. At that time, strangely enough, the population in Saigon still felt safe and secure.

Arriving at the office, Sam Longbottom told me that it would be better to take an early morning flight out the next day. He would get the money ready for me to take to Nha Trang.

On Friday morning Air America and Air Vietnam were busy evacuating people out of Danang. I would have to wait until Saturday morning for a flight back to Nha Trang.

At noon I went downtown to meet Long Pham at a restaurant for lunch. He appeared to be unusually tense. As he began to talk and relax, I found out the reason for his stress. He said that he had called the Danang air control tower shortly before coming for lunch, and a North Vietnamese voice had answered the phone. He hung up as he realized that the North Vietnamese had taken the Danang airbase. Early Saturday morning we received official word that Danang had fallen to the NVA.

With the news of the fall of Danang we were extremely concerned, not only about the people of that area, but in particular about two of our missionaries who were still in the Danang and Hue vicinity. There had been no word from them in several days. After several days of prayerful vigil, we were relieved to know that they were evacuated out of Danang on a ship packed with refugees.

It was a joyful sight to see Bob Davis and Gene Tunnell walk into our mission office once again. They related a harrowing story of being caught in the chaotic crush of trying to get out ahead of the NVA army, along with thousands of frantic Vietnamese. Even in the times of stress they were able to minister to the Vietnamese on the ship with them.

Early Saturday morning I decided not to return to Nha Trang. The planes leaving from Saigon for Nha Trang were empty. They were trying to evacuate as many people as possible from Nha Trang, before it fell to the advancing North Vietnamese Army.

Early Monday morning we heard that Nha Trang had fallen to the invading North Vietnamese Army. We caught a flight out to Manila that Monday afternoon. The country had collapsed so fast that it left us numb. Still feeling numb and bewildered, we flew into Manila.

Our time of missionary service in South Vietnam was over. The door was shut, but God would open other doors.

Regrouping in the Philippines

Leaving a tension-filled city and a country on the verge of collapse, we flew into Manila on 1 April 1975. Visiting the Philippine Baptist Mission office, an "Old China Hand" put the situation in perspective for us. "You're not the first missionaries to be forced out of a country, and you will not be the last." She was right about that.

We stayed overnight at the Mission guesthouse, and left the next morning for Baguio City. The previous year we had spent several nights in Baguio City while on vacation. It was the right place to stay until we had directions about where we would go next. The cool climate, beautiful flowers and rolling mountains made Baguio City an excellent place for rest and recuperation. The Philippine Baptist Seminary was located there. The guesthouse where we stayed was located on the campus of the seminary.

It did not take us long to get acquainted with the professors who taught at the seminary. Some of the younger professors' children were the same age as Joey and Anne-Marie. Gloria and I quickly found a warm fellowship between the American and Filipino professors.

Some of the ladies introduced Gloria to the shopping wonders of Baguio while I was introduced to the tennis court. It did not take long for me to discover that I was not on the same level of skill as the professors; however, I did enjoy the challenge of the game and the fellowship. I might add that little mercy was shown out on the court.

During our month stay in Baguio City, we had the opportunity to go out and visit in the churches. Dr. Grover Tyner, the president of the seminary, invited me to go out with students in view of starting a new mission on the outer edge of the city. That was an enjoyable experience as a church planter.

Earl and Mamie Lou Poesy introduced us to the student ministry. It was exciting seeing the enthusiasm and fervor of the Filipino university students.

Several days after our arrival in Baguio, Walter and Pauline Routh came up from Manila to Baguio. They had served in Quang Ngai Province in South Vietnam. When they evacuated out of Quang Ngai they left most of their household goods with us in Nha Trang. Their goods suffered the same fate as ours . . . lost forever.

They stayed at the guesthouse with us on the campus where we spent many hours together in fellowship and prayer. We listened to the radio as the Voice of America reported that the North Vietnamese were closing in on Saigon.

In the last few days before the fall of Saigon, Walter and Pauline returned to Manila. A few days later we heard that Walter had taken the last Pan Am flight back into Saigon. His purpose was to bring out any Baptist that he could get on a flight out. There was no one who could do it any better. Walter knew the city, and he was fluent in the Vietnamese language.

Barbara and Jim Lassiter, who were serving in Saigon before evacuation, were in Manila with Walter and Pauline. When Walter asked them who they wanted him to bring out of Saigon for them, they quickly answered, "Our helper, Bich Lin."

Upon arriving in Saigon Walter hooked up with Long Pham who was working at Tan Son Nhut as an air controller. Long's knowledge of the airbase and Walter's commanding presence, enabled them to get 48 Baptists together for one of the last flights out of Tan Son Nhut. Bich Lin was among those 48 Baptists.

It must have been past midnight when I was jarred awake by the continuous ringing of the telephone in the guesthouse in Baguio City. It was Walter. He had just arrived at Clark Air Base with the group of Vietnamese Christians.

He wasted no time in telling me what he wanted: "Joe, you gotta get down here! I'm here with 48 of our people, including Long. Flights are coming in every few minutes from Saigon. The place is falling apart. They need interpreters here. Come on down! I've gotta go."

The next morning we packed our suitcases, and caught a bus to Manila. Arriving in the middle of the afternoon, we checked in at the Manila Hotel.

After settling the family in, I caught a bus to Clark Air Base. On the way there, I was thinking about how exciting...meeting up with my Baptist friends, especially Walter and Long. I was thinking, also, how glad the Air Force would be to have me as an interpreter.

Was I ever in for a big surprise! Surprise number one: when the bus arrived at the Clark gate, everyone produced a pass that I did not have. The guard at the gate told me to get off the bus.

Going into the guard shack I explained to the Air Policeman on duty who I was, and that I had come to serve as an interpreter.

He said, "You'll need to talk to Major Brown and get his O.K. The phones are over there."

The phone was located about 20 yards inside the base. I called up Major Brown anticipating his warm response to my coming to help out.

Surprise number two: Major Brown said, without even a greeting: "We don't need you! We've got more people running around here than we need. Most of them don't know what they're doing. Goodbye!"

Standing by the telephone booth in a semi-shocked condition, trying to figure out my next move, I heard a voice saying, "Where are you going?"

A base bus had stopped about six yards from me. The driver seeing my startled and uncertain look, repeated his question, "Where would you like to go?"

I took a quick peek over toward the gate. The guard was busy waving cars in to the base. After all, he didn't know what Major Brown said. I told the bus driver, "I'm looking for the Vietnamese refugees."

"Get on" he said, "I'll take you right there."

Going into the barracks where the refugees were temporarily staying, I had a joyful reunion with Walter, Long and other Christian friends.

Walter took me over to meet the Colonel who was the head chaplain and highest-ranking officer working with the refugee project. He greeted me warmly and told me how glad he was to have me to help out with the refugees. I discreetly refrained from saying anything about Major Brown and how I got on the base. He gave me a large badge to wear that said, "Chief Interpreter."

He instructed me: "You're the authority in working with these people. You're in command. Whatever needs to be done, you tell them and it will be carried out."

I couldn't help but thinking: a short while ago I was a reject at the gate to the base. Now, I'm the chief authority in the refugee program. The Lord works miracles, His wonders to perform!

After working two days and nights with the refugees, with hardly any sleep, I received word that I was to meet Dr. Keith Parks, our Area Director, in Manila.

Working among the Vietnamese refugees, if only for a short while, was a gratifying time for me. Knowing something of the culture and language, I was able to help move them about without causing chaos. Feeling good about the time spent at Clark, I headed back to Manila to be with Gloria and the children, and to meet with Dr. Parks.

Just after arriving at the hotel, a tremor shook the building for a good 20 seconds. We had never experienced an earthquake or a tremor. It was scary.

A few minutes after the tremor there was a knock at our hotel door. It was Ed Gordon. Ed and his wife, Audrey, served in the city of Dagupan, which was about 30 miles north of Manila. He was at the seminary as a guest teacher while we were there.

Ed Gordon was one of the most joyful Christians that I've ever known. "Rejoice in the Lord always" was carried out daily in his life.

Ed invited us out for lunch.

Being on the eighth floor we took the elevator. While we were about half-way down, the power and lights went out. Bingo! We were stuck between the fourth and fifth floor. The children begin to cry. It was pitch dark and we were stuck in this very small space. Ed started to sing, "Praise ye the Lord, hallelujah!"

I could hear the Filipino workers in the elevator-building door above, telling one of us to climb out the door and hook a chain on something. Being the younger of the two men, I did it. The workers, then, manually pulled us up to the next floor.

That evening we met with Dr. Keith Parks, along with Bob and Priscilla Compher, and Jim and Barbara Lassiter.

After dinner together, he met with us by couples. Realizing that we were near furlough time, Dr. Parks suggested that we take a six-month furlough. Then, he asked us if we felt led to any particular country.

Without any hesitation we both said, "Indonesia." He suggested that we go on home, pray about it and let him know at Foreign Mission Week at Glorieta Conference Center in New Mexico.

During Foreign Mission Week at Glorieta, Gloria and I told Dr Parks that we felt led to serve in Indonesia. He said that he would notify the Indonesian Baptist Mission, so they could start to work on getting us visas.

He cautioned us, "You'll have to be patient. It may take a while to get your visas."

Dr. Parks was right about it taking a while to get our visas. We were in the process for a year and six months before we were to receive our visas. In the meantime, Dr. Parks had become the new president of the Foreign Mission Board, and Dr. Bill Wakefield became our new area secretary for Southeast Asia.

Dr.Wakefield suggested that we go on to the Philippines and wait there until we received our visas. He said that Dr. Grover Tyner, president of the Baptist seminary in Baguio City, had requested that we come and work with students at the seminary in helping them start new churches in the barrios.

Dr. Tyner met us at the airport in Baguio City. He was not one to lose any time for he had driven the old Chevrolet, that was to become our car, to the airport.

He said, "Joe, you come on with me. Libby can take Gloria and the children to the guesthouse. We can go on to the barrio where you'll be working with students to start a church. I'll introduce you to the Filipino leaders in the barrio."

The next ten months in Baguio City were memorable times. The most exciting time was the birth of our daughter,

Elizabeth Gayle. Elizabeth's joining our family was a real special time for her older eight year old brother, Joey, and big sister, seven year old, Anne-Marie.

Bill and Audrey Roberson, our dear friends who served with us in Vietnam, helped to name Elizabeth. They, like us, had transferred to the Philippines after the fall of South Vietnam. They were serving in Manila.

They were visiting in Baguio for a few days to find relief from the heat and congestion of the big city. On our way out to eat dinner one evening, we asked them to help us come up with some names for the coming baby.

As names came pouring out, Elizabeth and Gayle were connected, and we all agreed that Elizabeth Gayle should be the name if, indeed, the baby was a girl.

It was a girl, and Elizabeth Gayle became a beloved member of our family. Her first eight months were spent in beautiful Baguio City, Philippines.

During the second week in December 1976, we received word from Indonesia that our visas had been granted. We began to make plans for going on to our new country of service.

The first week in January 1977, we said goodbye to friends in the Philippines and boarded a flight for Jakarta. For the next twelve years we would have an exciting ministry in the beautiful country of Indonesia.

Hello, Hello Bandung

After almost a year in the Philippines we arrived in the lovely country of Indonesia to continue our work as church planters. Ed Sanders, the Indonesia Baptist Mission Chairman, and his wife Jaletta, met us at the airport.

After a two-day whirlwind tour of Jakarta where we met the members of the Mission serving there, Ed drove us to Bandung where we would study the Indonesian language. On the way to Bandung, Ed gave us a running commentary about Indonesia and the need for planting new churches. His passion for evangelism and love for the Indonesian people was obvious and contagious.

Ed had a special rapport with children, and to our delight, he made Joey and Anne-Marie feel special. Our eight-month old Elizabeth received her share of hugs and attention.

Arriving in Bandung we went directly to our apartment on Hegarmanah Street, which would be our home for the next year. We were happy to know that our neighbors would be Jim and Margaret Gayle who were in their sixth month of language study. They had been our nearest neighbors in South Vietnam. Rob and Janie Sellers, who were with us in the Philippines while we were all waiting for visas to enter Indonesia, were our next-door neighbors. Coy and Teresa Jones and their three children were the other couple living near by.

Our year in Bandung was a pleasant and memorable experience. We often gathered with the other families to eat, play board games and have quality fellowship time. There's a special bonding between missionaries studying the language together in a new country.

In February 1978, a special event happened in our family while we were in Bandung. Our youngest son, John

Mark was born at the Baptist hospital in Kediri. We all went down a week early to wait for the new baby's arrival. A guesthouse, near the hospital grounds, was available for us.

The anticipated day came and John Mark joined his two sisters, Anne-Marie and Elizabeth, and his older brother, Joey, in the Turman family. Dr. Kathleen Jones and Ruth Vanderburg were the attending doctor and nurse. This team had delivered many of our Indonesian Mks, and John Mark became another "Kediri baby."

The day after John Mark's birth, we were permitted, as a family, to go in to see him. At the nursery, there was a large glass window, and at a given time, they displayed all the new babies. As we approached the glass window, we saw that most of the Indonesians were gathered at one end of the long glass window. Looking for John Mark, we saw him at the end of the window, a little white baby lying there with all the beautiful brown babies. The Indonesians were staring at him, because most of them had never seen a white baby.

After Gloria and I had finished our language study we stayed an extra four months in Bandung waiting for our assignment to an area of Indonesia. During this waiting period I was "invited" to be the driver for a team coming from Texas to hold a revival in the First Baptist Church in Bandung.

Why are these guys coming here to hold a revival meeting? I thought. They don't know anything about the language or culture. Reluctantly, I said that I would be the driver for the team. After all, I did have a VW van that would be adequate to take the entire team of eight people.

This experience with a team of volunteers would forever change my perspective about volunteers coming to work with missionaries.

The Texas team consisted of the pastor, a tall, six-foot-four Texan who wore a Stetson and cowboy boots. He was triple talented as he preached, played the trumpet and sang specials. On the side he did counseling. The laymen and women, who came with him, were members from his church.

One of the ladies in the group, who was in her middle thirties, had just rededicated her life two months before the trip. Several in the group were Sunday School teachers. None of them had ever been overseas.

After meeting the team and taking them to their hotel, my doubt about their being of any use in Indonesia was compounded. However, these doubts were soon dispelled as the team swung into action.

From the start the members of the team began to relate and talk to the Indonesian church members through interpreters. They were Texas-friendly and had a genuine desire to get to know their Indonesian brothers and sisters in Christ. Their loving spirit and desire to relate were communicated to the Indonesians without words.

The church was nearly full for the first revival service. After that, it was standing room only. The team members gave testimonies; the tall pastor played the trumpet, sang and preached. The Indonesian loved it! People were saved each night of the meeting and there were numerous rededications.

During the day the team members went out with Indonesian church members to witness to prospects. Many Indonesians were converted in their homes from these visits and came to make public commitments of their faith in the revival meeting. The team from Texas really impacted the church.

In the following years of service, I promoted partnership teams coming to our area of ministry. They were always a blessing to our churches.

Out of the overflow of the revival at the First Baptist Church came a ministry to college students. Batara, Timbul and Sahat had served as interpreters for the team in going out to witness to prospects in the city. The boldness of the Texas team members had fanned the flame of revival in their hearts.

They came to me the day after the revival. "Pak Joe, would you work with us in witnessing to college students?" I agreed to do so.

These students had gone through the Navigator's Scripture memorization program and had been taught how to witness and to follow up on those won to Christ.

They thought that the college students would be more attracted and interested in their presentations, if a foreigner was on the team. Whether my presence helped to achieve this purpose or not, I don't know; however, it did affirm and give confidence to the team.

One of the first endeavors of the student team was to get permission to place a questionnaire in the student center of one of the major universities in Bandung. Campus Crusade used the questionnaire in evangelism. It starts by asking general questions about life's destinations and ends with a question about where one will spend life in the hereafter. The students who were interested in talking about this were to respond by giving their name and address.

During the next two months we followed up on the one hundred and forty-six responses to the questionnaire by sharing a personal witness with the majority of them.

Follow-up Bible study groups were formed from those who made professions of faith in Christ. Some Follow-up Bible study groups consisted of two or three students, and some of them had up to ten.

Many follow-up groups were active in the city to minister to those who came out of our ongoing evangelism program.

One of the university students who joined our witnessing team was Franz. Crippled by polio when he was five-years old, Franz lurched along in a cross between a hop and a shuffle. You would quickly forget his handicap when he engaged you with his smile and positive spirit.

One Saturday afternoon, I was to meet the team at the First Baptist Church to go witnessing to student prospects. At twenty minutes before the appointed time, a tropical downpour drenched Bandung. Even though it was difficult driving, I was determined to be at the church on time. With such a downpour I doubted if anyone had arrived at the church. Driving slowly on the street in front of the church, I strained to see if anyone had arrived at the church. I did not see anyone.

Just as I started to drive on, I saw some movement near the outside wall of the church. Someone was standing under the eaves of the building. I pulled into the churchyard and jumped out with my umbrella. It was Franz.

I called out to him over the sound of rain pounding the church roof, "Franz, how'd you get here in all this rain?"

Franz flashing that wide grin, "I came early to be sure that I'd be on time."

We waited until the rain was past. Apparently, no one else was coming. I asked Franz if he was willing to go with me to the area of Bandung that we had targeted for visiting. We would have to navigate up and down some difficult slopes as some of the student housing was on the hillsides.

Franz exuded confidence, "Pak Joe, I can do it!"

With that positive response we set out on our witnessing adventure. That afternoon we met three students with prepared hearts. They came from nominal church backgrounds in North Sumatra. They knew nothing of the new birth about which Jesus talked to Nicodemus. That afternoon they had the joyous experience of being transferred from the kingdom of darkness to the kingdom of light and life in Jesus Christ.

On the way back to drop off Franz, we sang choruses of praise and rejoiced in the great salvation in Jesus Christ our Lord. What a joyful time!

After dropping off Franz, I reflected on his faithfulness and desire to be a witness for Christ. He inspired me to make an effort to be a more faithful and enthusiastic witness for Christ. Even though student evangelism was exciting, I knew that church planting was to be my work. We were ready and anxious to get onto our new field of service.

There were several possibilities in Central Java. We would be exploring the opportunities of serving in that area.

Turmans in Temanggung

Often, missionaries just out of language school do not want to leave Bandung and go to their new stations of service. The cool climate, the nice school for Mks, forged relationships and some anxiety about starting all over again in a new place, are some of the factors in their not wanting to leave beautiful Bandung.

We, however, were ready and anxious to get to our new field of service. The time in Bandung had been a good experience, but we felt strongly the leadership of the Lord in going to Temanggung.

I had gone to Temanggung a month before our move as a family, and rented a house. The house was located a mile outside of the city and was semi-surrounded by rice paddies. It had been built by the county attorney for his family. They had never moved in because a workman had hanged himself in the house. They were afraid of the departed spirit of the man. That did not bother us at all.

It was a nice house with a large picture-glass window in the living room looking out toward Mt. Sumbing, looming in the not-so-far distance.

Not long after our move, Gloria organized our home school program. She had ordered the materials some months before and was prepared to teach Joey, Anne-Marie and Liz. Joey was in the sixth grade, Anne-Marie the fifth and Liz was in kindergarten.

They would start school at eight and go to one o'clock. They would, of course, have generous breaks to maintain their energy and interest level. It was a smooth running school. Serving as principal, I would come in at different times, when available, and give readings or special studies.

After lunch, the students would spend an adventurous afternoon playing around the house or exploring the outdoors. Sometimes they would have special projects to work on. From this perspective, I am amazed at how Gloria was able to teach three children and do such a good job with them. To this day, our children say that the most memorable time in their missionary childhood was living in Temanggung.

After getting moved and settled in, we began to explore our new home area. Behind our house were rice paddies and a fast-flowing shallow river with rocks and large stones in it. Joey and Anne-Marie quickly discovered that the river was a delightful place to play. After their school hours, they scouted out different areas for hiking. They named their hikes, the river, rice paddy, and railroad hikes. The railroad hike was going along an old railroad track that went through a beautiful and rugged countryside.

Often, as a family, we would hike up the slopes of Mt. Sumbing to visit one of the villages and talk to the people. Our children would draw a large crowd wherever we went, in the countryside, or in the town.

My job as a church planter was to work with national leaders in strengthening the existing churches and start new churches. A small church already existed in Temanggung. The church met in the home of the local leader, Pak Madiyono. Twenty-two members attended the services. Pak Madiyono worked for the local county government. Shortly after our arrival, I begin to help Pak Madiyono with the teaching and preaching services. He mentioned another group that had started up in the village of Danu Payang; however, over a period of time they had quit meeting together. He observed, "If we will give them some leadership, this group will start meeting again and will grow."

Going to Danu Payang was not only an evangelistic opportunity but also a cultural experience. There, for the first time, I became acquainted with the Javanese culture and language. It was a delight getting to know the people and becoming their friend.

The Bible studies were held in the evenings. Pak Madiyono and I would arrive around 7.00pm. Hot tea and chips would be served as we sat on a straw mat on the floor. People would begin to filter in, greet us, and take a seat. There was a continual flow of conversation about the happenings of the day, or past few days. Usually, the service started around eight and went to nine-thirty.

Then, again, there was the serving of more hot tea and a small snack. The conversation would become more animated and continue on to ten-thirty or eleven o'clock. No one was in a hurry.

Several months after moving to Temanggung, I knew I needed to study the Javanese language. Bahasa Indonesia is the national language of Indonesia. It started as a trade language, but grew through the years to become the dynamic language that it is today. On the contrary, the Javanese language has been used for centuries. The Javanese are proud of their language and use it in their homes and religious meetings. We were immersed in the Javanese culture and language.

Pak Suwoto, a retired schoolteacher, was recommended to be my teacher. He was a member of the Javanese Christian Church, and an excellent teacher. From the beginning, he would only use the Javanese language with me. At first, it was very irritating, but then, I began to understand more and more Javanese. He would take me to Javanese restaurants for lunch, so that he could teach me the names of the Javanese foods. We would go on long walks in the country, so he could teach me the names used in farming.

He helped me prepare my first sermon to be preached at the Javanese Christian Church. Pak Suwoto proudly introduced me to the congregation before I preached. My sermon was short. I doubt if anyone understood much of what I said, but they all were very gracious. Certainly, they were very happy that I would try to speak their language.

After the first year in Temanggung, eight of the young men in the village of Danu Payang wanted to be baptized. They stood in the evening service and made their profession of faith. Afterwards, Pak Madiyono and I counseled with them about their commitment to Christ. The second year, twelve more made commitments to Christ. Pak Madiyono was right when he said that the work would grow if we provided some leadership.

Soon, the house where we were meeting was getting crowded. The group that met in Pak Madiyono's house in town was growing, also, but slowly.

One afternoon, just after lunch, I was sitting on the living room couch reviewing my language lesson when there was a knock at the door. It was a local high school girl who was interested in learning how to speak English. I told her that Gloria was resting but she would be up in a few minutes if she wanted to speak to her. While she was waiting, I made casual conversation about where she lived and attended school.

Then, I asked her if she had ever thought about spiritual matters. She said that she had often thought about the things of God and would like to be a Christian; however, she did not know how to become one.

With such an opening I shared the Good News of Jesus Christ with her. Indra responded by opening her heart to receive Christ. She prayed fervently confessing that she was a sinner and asking the Lord Jesus to forgive her and receive her. Just when she finished praying, Gloria walked into the room. I introduced her as Indra, a new child of God.

Gloria did teach Indra English and, also, how to be a follower of Jesus. Indra came faithfully every week for her Bible and English studies. We became acquainted with her family and had an opportunity to have an input in their lives. After Indra graduated, she moved to Jakarta. We introduced her to Kebayoran Baptist Church and to Jaletta Sanders. Jaletta continued to disciple Indra.

While in Jakarta, Indra met and married a US serviceman, Bill Long. Today, Bill and Indra live in California where they are actively serving in a church with their two daughters.

A Time to Witness

Islam is the predominant religion in Indonesia. Every facet of the culture and language is influenced by this religion that was introduced by Arab traders in the sixteenth century.

We, as missionaries, tried to be sensitive to whom and where we shared the Gospel. Those who were devout Moslems could and would take offense at a Christian pastor or missionary coming into their village to evangelize their people. The Indonesian government was also sensitive about this issue.

For this reason, we, as missionary church planters, would not go into a village unless we were accompanied by a national brother, or had been invited by someone in the village.

During our second year in Temanggung, Batara, Timbul and Sahat came to spend some time with us. They didn't come just to visit, but, in keeping with their previous zeal, they came to work with me in evangelizing the area.

One morning we went out to villages that I had not yet visited since coming to that area. Our plan was to go into the villages and visit the kiosks in order to meet people. A kiosk was a small news-stand that sold not only newspapers, but also candies and snack foods. At the kiosk we engaged men in conversation and sought an opportunity to witness to them.

At this particular village, after we had shared with several adults, a group of children came up smiling and talking with us. Batara, Timbul and Sahat responded to the children in a positive way, laughing and kidding with them about school and life in the village. Then, as the children took to them, they began to share with them the story about Jesus.

Recognizing what was happening, I warned them that we should not try to evangelize children, especially in a new village.

Timbul retorted, "Hey, it's all right. Jesus said, 'Let the little children come to me and forbid them not.'"

About that time, I saw one of the men in the village come and take down my license plate number.

Two weeks later, after Batara, Timbul and Sahat had returned to their university in Bandung, I was summoned to the Kabupaten (District Chief) office. As I was sitting, waiting to be called in to see the District Chief, I remembered the man taking down my license plate number in the village.

The government could expel me from the country, I thought as I waited to be called into the official's office. Praying as I waited, I committed it to the Lord, "Lord, help me to be true to You in this meeting and to glorify You, no matter what happens."

Just as I finished breathing out my prayer, I was called to enter the District Chief's office. I was surprised to meet such a congenial official. After a few minutes of getting acquainted, he did get down to business. "Was that your car out in the village?" he asked.

"Yes sir, it was."

"Did you and your friends try to evangelize the children?"

"Yes, the university students with me talked with the children and told them a Bible story. I told them that it was not a good idea to talk to children about religion without their parents' consent. But you know university students. They're zealous, but they meant no harm to anyone."

To my relief, the Chief seem to accept my explanation. He stood up and walked over to a map of the county on the wall.

Come over here," he said, "I want to show you villages where you can go and villages where you cannot go."

He pointed out the villages that were strongly Muslim and other villages that were open to other religions.

After we were seated again, he ordered tea and sweets to be served. He began to ask me about my family and country. We had a long and pleasant conversation. Just as I was about to leave, he leaned toward me and smiled broadly.

I would like to come to your house and visit you and your family sometime. Would that be possible?"

Sir," I answered, "I would be very happy and honored for you to visit us."

Two weeks later, the District Chief came to our house for a visit. He stayed for more than two hours. We showed him pictures of America and other places that we had visited in the world. He enjoyed talking to our children and seemed to be fascinated by the fact that we really enjoyed living in Indonesia. He appreciated that I was studying the Javanese language, and seemed surprised that I could speak some at that time.

On his way out the door, he turned and said, "If I can be of any help, please let me know."

It was good to know that the District Chief was our friend.

After that experience, I only entered villages with a national Christian who, himself, knew someone in that particular village. Following this guideline, we started two new groups in villages that were open to us.

The Healing of the Grandfather

It was not a pleasant experience for me to attend the neighborhood meetings. I strained to understand what was going on. To make matters more difficult for me, Mr. Sutarto, my neighbor, made cutting remarks about me as a foreigner.

When Mr. Sutarto came to my house on a Saturday morning, he asked me to go with him to his home village to pray for his grandfather.

I had reservations about his request. I told him that I would think about it and let him know that afternoon. I could not understand why he wanted me to go and pray for his grandfather. He was a Muslim and I was a Christian. Muslims just do not ask Christians to pray for them!

I was suspicious of Mr. Sutarto. Was Mr. Sutarto attempting to get me kicked out of the country? With these questions in mind I talked it over with Gloria. She cautioned me about being too hasty in turning down Mr. Sutarto's request. "After all," she said, "the Lord may be in it. Let's pray about it."

We spread the matter out before the Lord. When Mr. Sutarto dropped by to check with me, I told him that I would go with him at two o'clock the next day.

Promptly at two o'clock the following day (Sunday), Mr. Sutarto knocked on our door. Opening the door, I was surprised to see not only Mr. Sutarto, but also six of our neighbors with him. I was thinking that Mr. Sutarto would come alone. I was not expecting a supporting cast of Muslim friends. My instant feeling of displeasure quickly melted before their warm enthusiasm. It was Sunday afternoon and they were looking forward to an interesting outing in the country.

The grandfather's village was seven kilometers out from Temanggung.

On the way to the village, I talked to Mr. Sutarto about his grandfather. He said that his grandfather was more than a hundred years old. I doubted him. Later on, as I talked to people in the village, and the grandfather himself, I believed that he was that old.

The grandfather said that he was a young teenager when the volcano, Krakatau, erupted. At that time, Krakatau erupted with such force that it was heard half way around the world. It caused a tidal wave that killed 10,000 people in Jakarta and thousands of others in the outlying areas. It was a major disaster in Indonesian history.

If the grandfather was twelve years old when Krakatau erupted in 1883, then he would have been one hundred and nine years old at the time (1980).

Actually, the old man was Mr. Sutarto's great-grandfather. He had taken Mr. Sutarto in as his own child after his father died.

Driving over a village dirt road, we arrived at the grandfather's village. His house was sitting on the highest point in the village in the midst of a coconut grove. As we approached the house, I could see that it was the largest in the village.

Arriving at the house, we were greeted by at least twelve of the sons, grandsons and great-grandsons. They ushered us into a large front room. We were served hot tea with different kinds of fruits and sweets.

In just a few minutes the room was full of kinfolks and neighbors. Everyone seemed to be in a jovial mood as they asked me about my family and my home country. I enjoyed telling them about Gloria and the children. I related several funny things that had happened to us in getting adjusted to

Temanggung. They laughed at my stories. I enjoyed myself, even though I was on a mission of mercy.

Mr. Sutarto brought me back to my mission when he asked, *"Sudah siap?"* He asked me was I ready. I knew what he meant.

He was saying, "Are you ready to pray for my grandfather?"

I arose from the table hoping that only Mr. Sutarto would accompany me back to the grandfather's room. My hoping was in vain, for everyone who could squeeze in, entered the small room where the old grandfather lay on his bed.

It was then that I found out why Mr. Sutarto had invited me to come and pray for his grandfather. Back in his younger days, the grandfather had known a Dutch missionary. Even though he was not clear about the Gospel, the missionary and the message had made a deep impression on him. After being bedridden for several months, the grandfather requested that his grandsons bring a Christian missionary, or pastor, to pray for him.

The grandfather peered at me from the bed as his grandson told him that I was a Christian missionary who had come to pray for him. He turned his leathery face toward me and mumbled thanks in the Javanese language.

As I prepared to pray for the grandfather, many people, standing five or six deep, were staring in the window. The sons, grandsons and great-grandson were crowded around the bed. The door way was jammed with people.

I was conscious that the village was Muslim. Realizing that I would be praying in the name of Jesus in the midst of Muslims, I shot up many emergency prayers.

"Well, here goes Lord," I prayed in my heart, as I placed my right hand on the grandfather's head. Lifting my eyes toward heaven, I prayed in the loudest voice possible, so that everyone could hear me.

"Lord Jesus, in years past this grandfather heard about You. Now, he wants me to pray for him in Your name. Lord Jesus, heal this grandfather. Restore him and give him more days that he may come to know You. Heal him, Lord, that through his healing he would glorify You and this village would come to know You. Do it Lord so that Your name would be glorified in this place. In Your glorious name, I pray, in the name of Jesus Christ. Amen."

After the prayer, Mr. Sutarto said to me, "My grand-mother is lying next door. She's ninety-two years of age and has been bedridden for over a month. Would you pray for her?"

Going to the grandmother's bedside, I prayed for her in the same manner that I prayed for the grandfather.

After the prayers for healing, we went back to the round table with a marble top, to drink coffee and coconut juice.

Before our group left to go back to Temanggung, the sons and grandsons brought me a large cluster of coconuts.

Several weeks later, Mr. Sutarto came to our door. During those past two weeks, I had attended a meeting in Semarang and had worked in evangelism projects in the villages around Temanggung. In my busy schedule I had temporarily forgotten about the grandfather. Now, seeing Mr. Sutarto, I was curious about his health.

Mr. Sutarto asked, "Can you go with me to the village? My grandfather wants to see you. Today is a holiday and I do not have school."

Mr. Sutarto was the principal of an elementary school.

I quickly responded to his invitation, "Yes, I can. I would like to see your grandfather."

On the way out to the village, Mr. Sutarto said nothing about how his grandparents were doing. He wanted me to see for myself.

Coming to the village, we parked just below the grandfather's house. Walking up the hill to the house, we came out from the coconut trees to find ourselves in the front yard of the house. There stood the grandfather in the yard leaning on his walking cane!

Mr. Sutarto turned to me and exclaimed, "The Lord healed my grandfather."

Going into the house I saw the grandmother sitting at the table. He said, "My grandmother is healed, also."

The sons, grandsons and great grandsons came to greet us. They invited us to stay for lunch. Mr. Sutarto said that they were going to kill chickens. Chicken was only served for special occasions out in the villages.

While the women prepared lunch, we men sat around the old Dutch round table with the marble top drinking tea and telling stories. It was a grand time.

I really wanted to share the Gospel with the grandfather. However, he only spoke Javanese, and at that time, I only spoke the national language, Indonesian.

Several weeks after I had been in the Grandfather's village, Batara, Timbul and Sahat came to work with me in evangelism. Coming back from a village we saw a young man hitchhiking. Batara said, "Give him a ride, Pak Joe, and we'll share the Gospel with him."

The trio warmly greeted the young man. After exchanging greetings and general information about one another, they shared the Good News with the young man.

He had a prepared heart. He said that he had heard some things about the Gospel, but had never had anyone to explain it to him.

Now, the Lord sent three young men who could explain the Gospel clearly to his open heart. After sharing a witness and answering his questions, I pulled over to the side of the road to pray with them as the young man gave his heart to the Lord.

I was in for a big surprise! The young man was from the grandfather's village. When asked if he knew the grandfather, he replied, "Oh yes, everyone does. He's more than a hundred years of age."

I asked him if he would go with us to the village and interpret from Indonesian to Javanese as I witnessed to the grandfather. He answered that he would be happy to interpret for me.

Returning to the village, I had the privilege of sharing the Good News with the grandfather through the young man serving as an interpreter. The grandfather said that for a long time he had a desire in his heart to know Jesus. When I invited him to pray repenting of his sins and inviting Jesus into his heart, he did so without any hesitation. After his prayer, he said, "Now, I know Him in my heart."

While I was witnessing to the grandfather, Batara, Timbul and Sahat were leading four of the grandsons to know Jesus as Lord and Savior.

A short time after the grandfather professed Christ, he went to be with Jesus. I was invited to his funeral.

As I looked down on his body, I could picture him in heaven saying to the Lord Jesus, *"Matur nyuwun, Matur nyuwun,"* Thank you, thank you, Lord Jesus."

Whenever I think of the grandfather, I think of God's mercy, grace and patience that does not want anyone to perish, but wants all to come to repentance and faith in Christ Jesus.

God responded to the old grandfather's desire to know Him by sending the most unlikely people, by the most unlikely way, into his life with the Gospel. May His name be glorified!

Living and Serving in Mystical Central Java

There's a flow to life in Central Java that is not obvious to the casual observer. In order for one to get into the flow of Javanese life he needs to be an attentive student of the language and culture. He must be alert to the habits and subtleties of everyday life.

You can see the flow of life in the way the farmer prepares his rice paddy with his wooden plow and water buffalo. He's doing it the same way his great-grandfather did it. You can see the flow as the farmer comes to the recently harvested rice paddy with his ducks following him in an orderly row. He plants his staff in the middle of the paddy. The ducks will stay around the staff all day eating the loose rice grains left by the harvesters.

In the evening, the farmer will return and pull out his staff. The ducks will all line up, by pecking order, behind him, and he will lead them home.

You will see the flow of Javanese life when they come together for a village meeting. They have their "pecking order," or line of authority. It's not a democratic meeting, as we know it. They have a "musjawarah" which is a combination of discussion, consultation, deliberation and negotiation. No one is left behind as they all come to a consensus about the matter they're discussing.

Perhaps, one of the most significant activities that show the flow of Javanese life is the Javanese gamelan. The gamelan is the sacred Javanese orchestra with its stringed instruments, gongs, cymbals and drums. It plays mystical haunting melodies that have been played for hundreds of years by the Javanese. Actors and actresses who act out their legendary stories often accompany the gamelan.

Nothing is more mystical than to be out on a moonlight night in Central Java and hear a gamelan performing in a village, or on a nearby hill, or valley.

It was in this flow of life in Central Java that we tried to live out and share the life-giving Gospel of Jesus Christ.

Often I would ride my bicycle to the village rather than take our VW van.

The village was located about five miles from our house. Riding the bicycle gave me the opportunity to stop at kiosks, small stores, and houses along the way.

Some of the prospects for our church in the village lived along the road that led to the village. If I were driving, I would seldom stop at the house of one of the prospects. When I rode my bicycle, I would leave in the middle of the afternoon in order to visit along the way.

Usually, I would arrive in the village around seven o'clock for the Bible study. When the Bible study was over, I would go out and get on my bicycle. Most of the younger men would accompany me. Other people in the neighborhood would come out to see me off on my bicycle.

What would happen became somewhat of a ritual. For each time, without fail, they would ask me, "Are you going to go home alone?"

The background behind that question is that the people in Indonesia, by and large, never go out at night alone. They're afraid of evil spirits.

Realizing the reason for this ever-asked question, I would somewhat dramatize my departure. I would pause until all were leaning forward to hear my reply. Then, I would set up straight on my bicycle and announce in a loud voice so that all could hear in the area. "I'm not afraid because I'm not going alone. Jesus Christ is with me, and He is greater than all the evil spirits in the world!"

Just after that declaration, I would pedal off into the darkness of the night. Providentially, I always returned to the village, so they knew the Lord Jesus had taken care of me.

We could see Mt. Merapi ("mountain that has fire") from our front yard. It is the most active volcano in the world. One night it had an unusually large eruption and sprayed out lava, smoke and ashes over the area.

Waking up the following morning, we discovered volcanic ash covering our front porch and yard. The eruption fallout shut out the sunshine for a day. It was like a blanket of fog had been thrown over our area. Seeing the sun shut out and a semi-darkness covering the land, many people were afraid that the end of time had come. This opened the way for us to share the Good News with many people.

The Indonesian people believe in spirits. For this reason, we could talk about the Holy Spirit, or the Spirit of God, and find an interest on the part of the listener. The Bible is a book about the activities of the Spirit of God among His people. Once the Javanese begin to read the Bible, they were enthralled by its powerful message.

Through the light of the Gospel of Jesus Christ, the Javanese began to interpret the spirit world around them in a different way. They found a new mystic adventure in following Jesus Christ. In the light of Christ Jesus, the mystical world of Java became a different world where He, Jesus, is Lord over all the spirits.

The day came when we were invited to leave Temanggung and serve in Medan, North Sumatra. We were sad, yet excited about the new land and adventures ahead of us. Our time in Temanggung was a happy time for our young and growing family.

We will never forget living and serving in mystical Central Java, but Medan, here we come!

Moving to Medan

How swiftly four years goes by! We worked, played, studied, entertained guests, and tried to adapt to a new culture and language in Temanggung. Now, our mission was asking us to move to Medan, North Sumatra. We felt a surge of excitement at the thought of serving on the largest island in Indonesia.

Our friends, Jim and Margaret Gayle, were serving in Medan. They told us many things about North Sumatra and the activities going on in that area of Indonesia.

Being on furlough at the time, we had opportunity to pray and to discuss the move to Sumatra. When the time came for us to return to the field, we had a conviction that Medan was the right place for us to serve.

Since we were excited about living and serving in Medan, we communicated this excitement to our children. They were looking forward to living in a new area of Indonesia.

Our two oldest, Joey and Anne-Marie, would be students at Jakarta International School. Liz and John would be enrolling at Medan International School.

For the first time, our family would be separated. Joey and Anne-Marie lived in a hostel in Jakarta together with a number of other Missionary Kids whose parents served in various parts of Indonesia. Edna and Leslie Smith, a wonderfull missionary couple, served as house parents at this hostel.

Moving to Medan was an adjustment for us. Temanggung was a typical slow moving Central Java town. The Javanese were soft spoken, polite and non-confrontational.

The Bataks of North Sumatra were a vigorous, loud and confrontational people. Often, on the city streets, traffic would be held up as two drivers engaged in a shouting match, or a fistfight.

The Bataks believed in being *"terus terang,"* which means being frank, straightforward and blunt. You did not have to wonder what the Bataks thought about you. Sooner or later they would tell you. A thick skin was helpful in living and serving among the Batak people.

Although they can be loud and confrontational, the Bataks are a loyal and warm-hearted people. Once they have experienced Christ in their lives, they are strong and aggressive witnesses for the Lord. They are bold and willing to take a stand for Christ in the places where they live and work. The Bataks are good evangelists and it was our privilege to serve among them.

Once again, Jim and Margaret Gayle would be the missionary couple living nearest to us. They had been our missionary neighbors in Vietnam. The Gayles moved out of their house in Medan to a small town some forty kilometers away to accommodate our coming. Their generous and helpful spirit made our adjustment to Medan a lot easier.

We worked together with Pastor Samosir and the leaders of the First Baptist Church in Medan. Our assignment in Medan was to work along side our national Christians in building up the church. We also were to be catalysts in starting new churches.

The First Baptist Church had been founded some fifteen years before our coming. The church building was located on a large lot in the main part of the city. Its close proximity to the city center and accessibility should have made it a growing and thriving congregation, but it was not. A small congregation met faithfully for all services; however, they were not reaching out. The pastor, a prayer warrior and godly man, emphasized prayer and Bible reading. His gift was not evangelism.

He did recognize that Gloria and I had the gift of evangelism. He allowed us the freedom to exercise this gift in and through the congregation.

We started evangelizing our own neighborhood. Our house was located near a university of more than five thousand students. I began to go out and meet students on the streets and in the small food stalls along the side of the streets. They were friendly and open to conversation.

One day while I was witnessing to a student, the Pastor's son came looking for me. He waited until I had finished witnessing and leading a student to receive Christ. I was glad that he, as one of the leaders of the young people in the church, was able to see the Gospel presentation. Hopefully, it would challenge him and, also, he would share with his dad that I really practiced what I preached. The times that I had been asked to preach at the church, I had challenged them to reach out as witnesses.

Usually, in the morning worship service at the church, we would have several visitors. We noticed that most of them did not return on the following Sundays. Gloria and I asked Pastor Samosir for permission to visit those who had visited our church. He encouraged us to do so. Inviting some of the members of the church to go with us, we began to make contacts with those who had visited our church in the past weeks and months.

Many of the people that we visited were not clear about their salvation. They were open and we shared with them how to receive Christ as Lord and Savior. Many of them made a commitment of faith in Christ. Most of the people that we visited had never been visited by anyone, from any church.

The majority of those who made professions of faith in their homes came to church and were baptized. Over a two-year period, many adults were baptized into the fellowship of the church.

The church came alive as more and more of the members became involved in evangelism. Two new groups were started in areas where our members lived. Soon there were six new mission churches started in the city of Medan.

Medan is a city of more than a million and a half people. We enjoyed living and serving in Medan, but something happened to move us out to work among the villages of North Sumatra.

The Tala Peta Call

My morning study time was interrupted by a sharp knock at the door. Two students from the nearby university wanted me to bring a devotional message to their Christian fellowship group at their Friday noon meeting. They said that I could anticipate speaking to twenty-five to thirty students. At noon, on Friday, the Muslim students went to their mosques, and the Christian students used that free time to meet together for Bible study and worship.

Arriving on campus at the appointed time, I was met by the two students who had invited me. They led me to the university auditorium. More than five hundred students were seated waiting for the program to start. Surprised, I looked at my hosts with a "what's going on here" look.

With a pleased look on his face, one of the host students said, "We invited everyone to come and hear you speak!"

While the singing was going on, I decided to change my message. I had come to bring a discipleship challenge to a small group of Christian students. Now, there was an evangelistic opportunity. That past Sunday morning, as a guest preacher in one of our churches, I brought a message on "You Must Be Born Again." The message was still fresh on my mind and heart.

After presenting the message, I had the students to bow for prayer. I invited those to pray with me if they wanted to open their hearts to Christ Jesus to experience the new birth. After the prayer, many students raised their hands to signify that they had made a commitment to receive Christ into their lives. Raising your hand, as a sign of your commitment to Christ, is a significant commitment in a nation that is mostly Islamic.

When the program was over, many students came forward to speak with me for a moment. One of the students was Jaya Tarigan. He said that he wanted to come to my house and talk with me. I gave him our address and invited him to come.

Two days later, Jaya came for a visit. He did not waste any time stating his purpose for coming. Leaning forward in his chair, he spoke with a passion, "Would you go with me to my father's village? They're lost and in darkness. They need the Gospel!"

Surprised at the intensity of his question, I slowly answered him, "Jaya, I would like to go with you, but I can't go now. I have something on my calendar every day until the first of the year. Come back the first week in January and I'll talk to you."

When Jaya left, he was obviously disappointed.

The first week in January, Jaya came again. He repeated his request with the same intensity as before. When I ask him about his father's village, he told me that he did not live in his father's village, nor did his father. They lived in a small town near Medan where his father was an elementary school principal. His father, grandfather and other ancestors grew up in this village.

Jaya had been saved three months before his coming to our house. After he had come into the Kingdom of Light, in Christ, he visited his father's home village. He recognized that the village was still in darkness. He wanted me to go with him to take the Gospel to his father's home village.

I told Jaya, "You come Saturday afternoon at two o'clock and we'll go to your father's village."

Later on I invited Edy Sinulingga to go with us. Edy was a senior at the same university where Jaya attended, although they did not know each other. Edy was a dynamic witness for Christ. He was a forceful speaker who preached the Gospel with power.

That Saturday afternoon, Jaya came at one o'clock. Edy came a few minutes later. Meeting in my office, we had prayer together and sang a few choruses. Getting into my four-wheel drive Toyota jeep, we left for the village. It was a three-hour trip over bad roads. After we had traveled thirty kilometers from Medan, the roads got narrower and the rain forest trees got taller. Banana and other fruit trees were common alongside the road.

In that part of North Sumatra there are several rivers meandering through the area. Nestled alongside the river-banks are dozens of villages. Each of these villages will house between six to eight hundred people. Although some of the people are Christians or Muslims, many of them are animists. The animists believe that spirits reside in natural objects such as large anthills or trees. They will lay offerings before these natural objects in an effort to placate the spirits.

Coming into the village of Tala Peta, we parked in front of a coffee shop. The average coffee shop in the villages of North Sumatra will have a dirt floor, grass thatched roof and bamboo mat sidings. The villagers grow their own coffee. After a cup of village coffee, you will not sleep for twelve hours!

While we were drinking a cup of coffee, a young man seventeen years old, Tinjau Sinukaban, came into the shop. He asked, "Who are you?"

We replied, "We're Good News people. We've come to bring the Good News of Jesus Christ to this village."

"I've heard something of the Gospel on the radio, but I'm not clear about it. Can you help me understand it?"

I looked at Jaya and Edy and nodded my head. They knew what to do. Immediately, they began to share the plan of salvation with Tinjau. After twenty minutes they knelt on the dirt floor with him. I joined them in prayer.

I've never seen anyone take to the Gospel like Tinjau Sinukaban! He repented of his sins with tears coursing down his cheeks. Oblivious to the presence of others, he poured out his heart-felt prayers to the Lord asking His forgiveness and asking Christ to come into his life.

After his prayer of faith, he bounded to his feet exclaiming, "I know all the people in this village. They need this Gospel. I can take you to them!"

At that moment I knew that Tinjau would become a member of our new Gospel team. He did take us to the people in his village.

I asked Tinjau, "Where are the people? I don't see many people."

"Most of the people have not come in from the fields yet. In a few minutes you will see both the men and women come in from their fields. The women will go home and prepare the evening meal, and the men will go to the coffee shops."

Then, Tinjau added, "When the men come to the shops, we can witness to them."

That evening we did witness to a number of men in the coffee shops, and two men professed Christ.

Edy, Jaya and myself decided that we would come back to Tala Peta every Tuesday and Thursday afternoon after the young men finished their classes. Tinjau was excited about our plan to come back every week.

The next Tuesday evening we returned to the coffee shops in Tala Peta to witness to the men in the village. Many of the men were open and we led them to experience Christ in their lives. After a man openly professed Christ as Lord and Savior, he would, usually, invite us to come to his house for a meal. We happily accepted these invitations for it gave us an opportunity to share with the wife and family.

As the weeks past, we brought more and more people to know the Lord. Soon, we had sixteen people who were ready to be baptized. Something wonderful happened to bring the number up to eighteen.

Tinjau and I were witnessing to a man named Salam Barus in a coffee shop. During the middle of our presentation, he stopped us saying, "This message is too good for the coffee shop. Come to my house and share it with me."

We followed Barus to his house. After his wife served us hot tea, we finished witnessing to him. Tears flowed down as he confessed his sins and confessed Christ as Lord. Getting up from his knees, he asked us, "Would you share this with my father? He's getting old and he needs to hear this Good News."

We quickly voiced our willingness to share with his father. Salam Barus went next door and brought his father to us. We shared the Gospel of Jesus with him.

Toward the end of our presentation, the father said, "Many years ago, I knew a Dutch missionary who shared with us the Gospel that you're telling me about now. But I was never clear about the Good News. Tell me, is Jesus able to forgive me of all my sins?"

Tinjau and I had the joy of emphatically affirming the power of Jesus to forgive sin, "Yes, Jesus can and will forgive you of all your sins. Trust what Christ did for you on the cross!"

Then Grandfather Barus received the Christ that he first heard about some thirty years before.

The older Barus and his son, Salam Barus, were baptized along with the sixteen other villagers. They became the charter members of the Tala Peta Baptist Church.

Just recently when I returned to the village of Tala Peta after sixteen years, Yohan Kaban, the father of Tinjau, is now one of the main leaders of the Tala Peta Baptist Church. The church is sending teams into other villages in an effort to start new churches. They just purchased a plot of land to build a new church building, kindergarten and training center.

What about Tinjau Sinukaban? Tinjau is the pastor of Good News Baptist Church on the island of Batam. The church has nine full-time evangelists on a team that is evangelizing other islands in the area. Tinjau is still excited about sharing the Gospel of Jesus Christ!

Gospel Fire Out of Control

Once the Gospel got a hold on Tala Peta, it was bound to spread out of control . . . and it did. Some of the new believers at Tala Peta had relatives and friends in the neighboring village of Rumah Deleng. Soon, Rumah Deleng was inviting us to bring the Gospel to their village.

A team composed of Jaya, Edy, Tinjau, Johan Kaban and I went to Rumah Deleng. Following our method of evangelism that worked in Tala Peta, we went to the coffee shops. There we began to win men to the Lord. Some of the women from Tala Peta came over to witness to their wives. After six weeks we baptized our first group at Rumah Deleng and formed them into a church.

One man in the village who had been a believer for several years became the leader of this church. It began to grow slowly but steadily.

After the Gospel had taken hold at Rumah Deleng, some of their leaders wanted us to go with them to evangelize the village of Namulinting. Their friends at Namulinting had invited them to come with the Gospel.

Our team, with two men from Rumah Deleng, went to the village of Namulinting. Going to the coffee shops, we shared with the men in the village. The first evening three men professed Christ. One of the men who received Christ invited us to come back and hold meetings in his house. He was one of the village elders.

The Gospel was off to a good start at Namulinting. After several months, we baptized a large group of believers, both men and women, in the river near Namulinting.

Every week we were receiving invitations to enter new villages. A man from the village of Nyambe invited us to come his village with the Gospel. Our Gospel team headed for Nyambe. We had to park the jeep at Namulinting, and cross over a narrow sixteen-inch footbridge that spanned fifteen feet high over a river. One slip, in crossing over the footbridge, and you would end up in the river below.

The Indonesian team members walked across the bridge like they were walking across their front yard. When they offered to lead me across, I would have none of that. I always started praying about crossing the footbridge in the morning before crossing in the evening. It was really tough crossing in the evening when it was dark. We had only one lantern for our team of six people. They did let me walk across just behind the lantern.

After crossing the footbridge, we went a kilometer to another river that we had to wade across. We pulled off our trousers and shoes and held them over our heads as we crossed the waist-deep river. Walking another four kilometers across hills and valleys, we came to the village of Nyambe.

The village leaders greeted us warmly. They served us coffee and chips. Just as we finished drinking our coffee, a torrential downpour came. The downpour lasted for more than an hour.

Even though it was hard to hear with the rain pounding down on the tin metal roof of the village assembly building, we presented the Gospel message by picture and word. The people listened attentively. They were open to our coming and the message.

When the rain slacked off somewhat, the village leader told us that we had better start back, or we wouldn't be able to cross the river. He said that when the waters from up the mountain reached the river here, then it would become a swollen, swift torrent that would be impossible to cross.

We started out in the rain at a trot, for the village leader said that if we didn't make it across in the next fifteen minutes, or so, then we would have to spend the night in the village. We knew our families wouldn't know what happened to us, if we had to spend the night. With this in mind, we moved at a quick pace.

Coming up to the river, we could see that it was already swollen with a strong swift current. Pak Simatupang, who had just joined our team, suggested that we join hands and try to get across. He led the way, and I was the anchorman.

When we came to the middle of the river, I could feel the strength of the fast-moving current pushing against my legs and body. Both Jaya and Tinjau shouted that they were swept off their feet. They were holding on desperately. For a few scary moments that seemed like an eternity, I thought we would all be swept down the river. Then, we stabilized and walked through to the other bank.

Just a few months ago, I went back to North Sumatra. One of the team members at that time, Pastor Tinjau Sinukaban, was with me. Pastor Tinjau and I went back to Nyambe and the other villages that we evangelized in the eighties. Many of them have strong churches now.

When we came to the river that we crossed that night (it now has a bridge across it), we talked about our joining hands to get across the flooded river. Both of us mentioned how important it is for us in God's Kingdom, to "join hands" to carry out God's Commission in evangelizing a lost world.

By joining hands with the purpose of carrying the Good News to the lost of the world, the "Gospel Fire" will spread over the world.

From my recent visit, I found out that the "Gospel Fire" is still spreading in and among the villages of North Sumatra.

Going to the Far Ends of the East

On Thursday evening, as we were teaching new believers in Salam Barus's house at Tala Peta, a stranger came in and sat down in the back. When the teaching was over, he stood up and introduced himself as Mr. Tarigan from the village of Tanjung Timor.

He went on to say, "We don't have a Mosque or Church in my village. Would you come and bring the Gospel to Tanjung Timor?"

We, as a Gospel Team, quickly voiced that we would come to his village

Six weeks passed by and we did not go to Tanjung Timor. We meant what we said, but our involvement in starting new groups in Rumah Deleng and Namulinting took most of our time.

Mr. Tarigan, again, came to our Thursday night meeting. After the teaching was over, he stood up. This time he pointed to me saying, "Why haven't you come to Tanjung Timor?"

He pointed to me, because I had the vehicle, a four-wheel drive Toyota jeep that could make it to Tanjung Timor. Feeling somewhat embarrassed that we had not come to his village; I was slow in answering him.

Seeing my hesitation, he quickly added an assertion: "We deserve to hear the Gospel also!"

His emphatic statement impacted me. Yes, they did deserve to hear the Gospel because Jesus died for every person in Tanjung Timor.

I quickly told him, "We'll come to your village this Saturday." The Indonesian team members all nodded their approval.

Jaya, Edy and myself, left Medan at 4:00 am. on Saturday morning. We arrived in Tala Peta at 6:30 am in time to have breakfast with Tinjau, Yohan and Salam Barus. After breakfast we all piled into the jeep and took off for Tanjung Timor.

Undoubtedly, the road to Tanjung Timor is one of the worst in the world. Potholes two feet deep and four feet wide were frequent along the way. In spite of the four-wheel drive jeep we were stuck four times. The pushing power from the men with me kept us on our mission. We arrived in the village several hours before sundown.

After bathing in the river near the village, we were invited to eat with one of the families.

The village chief and elders came to meet us. They told us that they had called the people to meet together in the village assembly place in the middle of the village. The meeting was to be at seven o'clock.

In Indonesia, especially in the villages, they go by "jam karet," that is, "rubber time." Seven o'clock means anytime between seven and eight o'clock.

The people turned out for the meeting. The village chief said that almost everyone was in attendance. The village population was eight hundred plus people.

The village chief introduced the team. I made the appropriate remarks and turned the program over to our Batak Karo speakers. Edy Sinulingga, Jaya Tarigan, Tinjau Sinukaban and Yohan Kaban gave salvation testimonies and teaching on God's provisions for us in Jesus Christ.

Jaya and Tinjau gave a storytelling approach to sharing the Good News using pictures to illustrate the stories. The program lasted for three hours. No one left during the three-hour presentation.

After the meeting, the village chief and elders told us that they would meet with us in the morning.

We were invited as a team, to spend the night with one of the families in the village. The family was gracious and hospitable.

The usual house out in the Karo villages has a large front room for receiving and sleeping guests. There are smaller rooms in the back where the family members sleep. Some of the houses are made from wood while others will have grass-thatched roofs with platted bamboo mats for the siding. The floors are often dirt floors. There is such a thing as a "clean dirt floor." These dirt floors were hard and kept very clean by continual sweeping.

When guests come, the host and hostess would spread a bamboo mat over the floor for the guests to sit on. The same mats would be used for the guests to sleep on, if they spent the night.

That night the hostess spread a large bamboo mat on the ground floor for us to sleep on. In order to facilitate getting to sleep on a ground floor, I took several aspirins to relax my back. I passed the aspirins around for the team members.

The first time I took aspirins out in the village, without offering any to my fellow team members, they felt slighted. So each time I took an aspirin, I routinely passed them to the team members who were always anxious to take one.

That night, the host and hostess, seeing me pass around aspirins, held out their hands for one. The windows and door were still open with around ten or twelve people looking in. Their hands came poking in as they saw the aspirins being handed out. I emptied my aspirin bottle, giving one to each person.

I'm sure it made them feel better, because every time I returned to the village they wanted an aspirin.

Getting up with the village at 5.00am, we went to the river and bathed. Returning to our host house, we ate a breakfast of steamed rice, fried eggs and strong black coffee.

The village chief sent a messenger inviting us to come to his house. At the chief's house we sat in a circle with him and the village elders on a mat in his front guest room. His wife served us hot tea.

The chief and the elders asked us questions about the meaning of salvation and how one can become a Christian. This question and answer period lasted almost an hour.

Then, after an interlude of silence, the village chief stood holding his hand over his heart. He professed: "I receive Jesus Christ in my heart as my Lord and Savior."

He sat down and each one of the village elders stood and made their profession of faith. Then, the chief rose again saying, "This village will receive Jesus Christ as their Lord and Savior."

We knew what he meant. He was saying that by his example and influence, and that of the elders, most people in the village would become believers in Christ.

Our team made many more follow-up visits to Tanjung Timor. The majority of the people in the village did profess Christ as Lord and Savior. Tanjung Timor was a difficult village to travel to, but it was one of the most rewarding experiences of my missionary career.

The people of Tanjung Timor did deserve to hear the Good News of Jesus Christ!

Pak Sim's Commitment

He was an Indonesian of Chinese descent. Tall, with a balding head, Pak Sim was a singular figure on his block. When we first came to Medan he made an effort to get acquainted with us. He, his wife, and single daughter, lived above their shop in the downtown area of Medan. Being fluent English, he chose to speak English with us rather than Indonesian. From the beginning, he let us know that he had a special affinity for Americans and wanted to be friends with us.

Soon after our arrival we were invited for dinner with Pak Sim and his family. At that time he told me that he was interested in reviving a Chinese speaking church in the Mandala area of Medan. He wanted me to help him. I told him that I would, but first, I needed to get acclimated to Medan and the work with the First Baptist Church.

Several months later he mentioned to me, again, the need to revive the Chinese church work. I told him that I would bring the matter up with the pastor and the leaders of the church.

At the next opportunity, I discussed Pak Sim's request with Pastor Samosir and the deacons of the church. They were enthusiastic about the possibility of me working with Pak Sim in the Mandala area. They saw the need for the church to be revived as it had stopped holding meetings some time before.

The family, who were the prime movers in the church, were still holding meetings in their home. They wanted someone to help them get the church started again.

Mandala was located in a thickly populated area of Medan. Most of the inhabitants were Chinese-Indonesians who spoke the Hakkien dialect. Many of them had fled from the fanatical Islamic Province of Aceh in the sixties when riots broke out against them. Hundreds were killed and their homes and stores were burned down.

They were a tight community that had little to do, socially, with the indigenous Indonesian population. Although they had to deal with Indonesians economically, there was no mutual bond of trust between them.

The Northern Province on the island of Sumatra is unusual for Indonesia; in that fifty percent of the population is Christian. Most of the Christians are from the Batak tribe.

The Chinese and Bataks seem to bond together as they have a mutual respect for one another. As Pak Sim and I began to go to Mandala to try to revive the church, several Bataks worked with us.

The first thing we did was to survey the area. Pak Sim introduced me to the Chinese he knew in the area. We walked around the neighborhood talking to people and trying to discover some of their interests and needs.

The Chinese young people were keenly interested in studying English. They seem to be the most open group to us. Pak Sim suggested that we start an English program for those interested.

Starting an English program would involve having a facility. Mrs. Ai Hong, the mother of the family holding meetings in their home, knew of a house in the middle of the area that was for rent. She talked to the owner and he was willing to rent it for a reasonable cost. The Ai Hong family had saved their tithes and offerings, so we had enough money to pay the rent.

We publicized our English program as well as our worship service that was to be held in the rented house. The English program got off the ground quickly as we enrolled twenty-five students. Studying English generated a lot of enthusiasm in the neighborhood. Our worship service grew from twelve people to more than twenty in regular attendance.

Pak Sim was always there, encouraging us and the other members. He served as the church treasurer and did whatever needed to be done. When I was out of town, he was the contact for the guest preacher and leader of the worship services.

He often went out to Mandala alone to find out what was really going on in the lives of the members and community. He spoke their heart language, Hakkien. After these visits he would have a conference with us about how to improve the ministry to the community and the worship services.

Our worship services at Mandala were on Sunday evenings. Often, I had just returned from working in the village. Pak Sim knew when I was gone to the village for the weekend.

He would call our house around three o'clock Sunday evening and say, "Pak Turman, are you ready to go to Mandala? We need you."

I never was able to say no to Pak Sim, even though I was dead tired from spending the weekend in the villages. I knew he was totally committed to growing a strong church at Mandala.

In July 1988 we were forced to leave Indonesia along with many of our fellow missionaries. Several weeks before our departure, I preached at a base camp in Aceh Province for the Mobile oil workers. One of the families in the congregation asked if we needed a nice organ for our church. They said it had been used in the English service for expats in Medan several years ago, but it now, was not in use. We quickly affirmed that we could use it, having Mandala in mind.

After the house was packed up, Gloria and the children went on to Semarang where we would, later on, meet together as a family. I stayed in Medan to finalize our household goods and get them loaded on the trucks. Shortly before I left, I called Pak Sim and told him that I had a surprise for him and the church at Mandala. Loading the organ into our van I took it to Pak Sim's house.

I've never seen anyone so delighted with a surprise! He beamed with joy upon seeing the organ.

He said, "I can hardly believe it! This is exactly what we need for our church. Pak Turman, you have blessed us! You must come back and visit us soon."

Gloria and I did go back to visit the church at Mandala twelve years later, in January 2000. There was a touch of sadness as we entered the neighborhood, for Pak Sim was not there. Several months after we left Medan, a motorcycle hit Pak Sim as he crossed the street in front of his house. He died instantly. As I looked down a street at Mandala, I could almost visualize the tall, singular figure of Pak Sim striding along, with purpose... committed to building the church at Mandala.

Closed and Open Doors

In July 1988, our visas to Indonesia expired and could not be renewed. We would have to leave Indonesia. This was also true with many other missionaries serving in Indonesia at that time.

Our Area Secretary, Jerry Rankin, asked us if we would serve an interim year at the Baptist Student Center in Baguio City, Philippines. The prospect of working with students in the Philippines was exciting. After prayerful consideration we said yes to the invitation.

This was an assignment that appealed to us, but we didn't want to make a commitment based solely on our desires and excitement. We wanted to have an affirmation of God's leadership in going to this new assignment. The door was open and we did feel led to enter it!

Living in Baguio City was not a new experience for us. After being forced out of Vietnam in 1975, we lived in Baguio for almost a year. Our daughter, Elizabeth Gayle, was born there in May 1976. So, we were familiar with Baguio City and had good memories of it. It didn't take long to get settled in and start our new ministry.

Working with college and high school students was exciting and challenging. There were twelve Filipinos on the student center staff. Six of them were experienced workers having served with the Center for several years.

Our predecessors, Earl and Mamie Lou Posey, had led the student ministry for more than twenty years. They were highly respected by their colleagues and the students. Through their innovative ministry, the Baptist Student Center had become a well-known and an effective institution in the city.

Our first meetings with the staff were for times of Bible study and prayer. We wanted to get to know them and have a time of sharing together. Out of these meetings we hoped to set priorities for the coming school year. Gloria and I were pleased with the priorities that came out of this sharing time.

The priorities were: 1) to witness to as many students as possible in the power of the Holy Spirit and leave the results of the witness in the hands of God. 2) To follow up on every student who receives Jesus Christ as Lord and Savior and endeavor to get them involved in a Bible study and a Bible-centered church.

Several months after our arrival in Baguio, Gloria and I, along with our staff, went through a "Great Commission Workshop." The workshop materials were from the creative materials of Campus Crusade. The workshop revived us, renewed our vision for reaching students with the Gospel, and sharpened our skills in personal witnessing.

Out of this workshop came some changes in the way we were doing our programs at the Center. First of all, we did not open the Center until 10:00am. Each of us staff members were to be on a campus from 8:00-10:00am.

We mutually decided who would go to which campus. Our purpose was to share a witness with as many students as possible.

At 10.00am two of the staff members opened the Center to receive students who came for follow-up sessions, or to use the library. Our programs were structured in such a way as to be used for witnessing opportunities. The key to these changes was the personnel who were eager to witness and were looking for opportunities to share Christ with the students.

On a beautiful sunny morning, instead of going to the campus, Gloria and I decided to go to the lake, which is located in the center of downtown Baguio City. Many students went to the lake to study when the weather was nice. Approaching the lake, I suggested to Gloria that she go one direction, and I would go the other.

While on the way around the lake, I saw a park bench. Sitting down I prayed that someone would join me. A student in his early twenties came and sat down. Greeting him, we talked about the nice weather. Then, I asked him if he ever thought much about spiritual things. He replied that he often did. I asked him if I could share some spiritual truths with him.

After giving me permission, I shared the Good News of Jesus Christ with him. At the close, I asked him if he would commit himself to Christ as Lord and Savior. After he said that he wanted to, I asked him to pray as a way of opening his life for Christ to come in.

He said, "Pray here?"

"Yes," I said.

"Why not," he enthused, before he prayed a heartfelt prayer asking for God's forgiveness and for Christ to come into his heart.

After his prayer, I went through the verses of assurance with him and invited him to attend one of the follow up classes at the Center. He said that he very much wanted to attend a class.

The next morning he did attend a follow-up session. After that, we never saw him again. We assumed that he was one of those who were insincere in their commitment.

This happened in May. In August we went to the States on furlough. That following March I received a letter from this student that was forwarded from the student center in Baguio. In his letter, the student explained to me that he had dropped out of school because of financial reasons and was now on a Greek ship.

He thanked me for sharing the Gospel with him and concluded by saying, "Please pray for me as I'm leading a Bible study on ship."

This experience only confirmed that we are to bear witness to the saving power of Jesus Christ wherever we go, and leave the results to God.

During the afternoons we had follow up classes for those who made professions of faith. The high school groups, also, had their programs in the afternoons.

Friday evenings were set-aside for the university students to have their rallies. These rallies were always a high point of the week for the Center. Spirited singing, stirring testimonies and a challenging message were the usual program for the rallies. The assembly area at the Center was usually packed out for these meetings. Hundreds of students made commitments for Christ in these rallies.

In August we went on furlough after being in Southeast Asia for almost five years without a furlough break. We felt that our year in Baguio City had been fruitful, as well as exciting. Many students had come to profess Christ as Lord and Savior and had gone through the follow-up sessions. Some of them were already, at that time, emerging as Christian leaders.

At the Baptist Student Center in Baguio City many seeds had been sown. Some were bearing fruit. Our Lord, in a moment of time, in His providential grace, used us to be sowers of seed.

Called to David Livingstone Country

While on furlough in 1989-90, we felt led to explore the possibilities of serving in Africa. Knowing very little about the continent of Africa, we begin to read books and to ask questions. We discovered Africa was very open for missionaries to work with the national churches. But where would we go in Africa?

A missionary friend suggested that we call Zeb and Evelyn Moss. They had served in several countries in Africa over a period of more than twenty-five years. Calling them, we asked, "If you could choose any place in Africa to serve, where would you go?" Without any hesitation, they replied, "Livingstone, Zambia."

Putting Livingstone, Zambia on our spiritual radar screen, we began to pray seeking God's leadership about serving in that area of the world. We asked several churches to join us in praying about our going to Zambia. In the meantime, several events were taking place in Zambia.

The Moise-O-Tunya Baptist Church (The Smoke That Thunders Baptist Church) was a small and struggling congregation in Livingstone. They had survived over a period of ten years after Baptist missionaries, Lonnie and Fran Turner, were forced to leave because of the war situation in Southern Rhodesia (now Zimbabwe).

In the same time frame that we were talking to Zeb and Evelyn, the Moise-O-Tunya Baptist Church contacted the Baptist Mission of Zambia to request that a missionary be sent to help them.

Since the departure of Lonnie and Fran, the Moise-O-Tunya Church had moved from place to place in a desperate effort to survive as a congregation. In the early eighties the city of Livingstone had given them a large plot of land for building a church. Now, after ten years, the city said that they had to build within the year, or lose the plot of land.

The Zambia Baptist Convention requested that the Baptist Mission of Zambia send a missionary couple to work with the Moise-O-Tunya Church. The Baptist Mission sent a request to Richmond. All of these actions happened over a period of several weeks. It usually takes months for missionary personnel requests to clear all the desks, but all of these events came together at the right time and resulted in our going to serve in Livingstone, Zambia.

In September 1990, we left for Africa and made our first stop in Nairobi, Kenya. From Nairobi we drove to Rift Valley and left Elizabeth, our fourteen year-old, at her new school. Liz was looking forward to boarding school. She met her new roommates and seemed to happily adjust to her new surroundings. Leaving her was difficult for us because she was our darling Liz who had always been with us. She sensed our concern at leaving her. She kept saying, "Don't worry, Dad and Mom. I'm all right. I already like it here."

Liz did make the adjustment to RVA. She graduated in 1994. While in Kenya, Liz climbed Mt. Kenya, Mt. Kilimanjaro and became a licensed scuba diver.

She continued her education at Samford University in Birmingham, Alabama where she graduated in 1998. She just recently graduated from Regent College in Vancouver, B.C. At the present time she is working with immigrants in Burlington, Washington. Oh yes, even though she was born in the Philippines, she considers herself to be an African MK.

John Mark, our youngest, continued on to Zambia with us. He was an alert twelve year-old who would be home schooled as a seventh grader.

Arriving in Lusaka we were warmly welcomed by the missionaries. We would be responsible for finding our own house in Livingstone. After several weeks in Lusaka where we checked in with the government offices and went through our missionary orientation, we went to Livingstone to look for a house.

Lonnie and Fran Turner took us to Livingstone. Having previously served in Livingstone, they were familiar with the area. On the way to Livingstone, I was shocked to see how dusty, dry and dead-looking the landscape was around us. No green was to be seen anywhere. This was such a contrast to us, after serving in Southeast Asia for twenty-three years, where the rich green luxuriant trees and plants stay green the year round.

Lonnie, seeing the shocked look on our faces, explained, "Everything looks so dead in the dry season; however, when it rains, everything turns into beautiful green, with flowers and plants shooting up. A wonderful transformation takes place."

We found this to be true, and came to appreciate the beauty of Africa. There is a wonderful wildness and beauty to Africa that is not found anywhere else in the world.

Driving through the city of Livingstone we continued toward Victoria Falls where we would spend the night in a hotel located near the Falls. About a mile from Victoria Falls, we had a "first." A herd of elephants crossed the road in front of us. It was at that time that we realized we were in the "real Africa." We were ecstatic at being so close to a wild herd of pachyderms! Even Lonnie and Fran, who had been in Africa for years, were caught up in the excitement of the moment.

The next day we met the pastor and other church leaders. They were eager for us to come and work with them. Their enthusiasm about our coming made us anxious to start the moving process to Livingstone. Later on that day, we did make contacts that led to us renting a house on the Maramba River, three miles outside of Livingstone.

Returning to Lusaka, we repacked our suitcases and moved to Livingstone. Driving toward our house by the Maramba River, we took the wrong fork in the road. Ending up at a house on a dead-end road, we inquired about directions. A British citizen with a Zambian wife came out to give us directions. He told us that we should go back and take the left fork.

Then, noticing John Mark, he fervently advised him, "Lad, don't be climbing around on these trees. Boomslangers hang out in them. Be careful playing around the ravine down below here. It's full of Egyptian cobras. Don't go wading around in the river. Crocodiles are in almost every body of water. When you get up in the morning, shake out your shoes. You may have a scorpion or spider."

Returning to get on the left fork, Gloria glanced toward me with an anxious look on her face, "You know, I never realized, until now, how wild Africa really is. There are so many ways to die here."

We cleaned up our newly rented house and moved in the next day. It had not been lived in for two years. All kinds of crawling and creepy creatures had moved in during the absence of humans.

Our British friend was right about the cobras. We almost stepped on cobras twice in our yard. The Zambians advised us to get dogs and cats and to cut all the weeds and grass around our house. We did that and were not bothered again with cobras.

Settling in our new house, Gloria and I began to study the Tonga language. John Mark started his Calvert course of study for the seventh grade. Tonga was our third language. We began the study of Tonga with the same excitement with which we studied the two previous languages. Learning a new language is an important part of the process of getting to know the people and culture. We knew from experience that getting the language is a must for becoming an effective missionary.

David Livingstone spoke several African languages. He was an example for us as we served in the land that he "discovered" for the Western world.

Building in Spite of Being Stumped

Growing up in rural East Texas I often heard people say, "I was stumped." Without knowing the history of the word I knew that it meant to be frustrated or baffled in your effort to make progress.

"To be stumped" is a colloquial expression that came from our forefathers who cleared the land of trees to plant their crops. After cutting down the trunk of the tree, they had to get the remaining part of the tree out of the ground. Getting the stump out of the ground could be a formidable task. With the limited tools available during that time, the farmers often had a stump that would not budge. They were "stumped."

I began to understand this expression more when we were "stumped" in trying to clear a plot of land to build a church in Livingstone. The church was given a plot of land by the city. By the time we arrived, ten years had passed and they had not been not able to finance the construction of a church building.

The congregation had moved from place to place over the ten-year period. When we came to worship and work with them they were meeting in the Presbyterian Fellowship Hall. Several months later we were forced to move to a room in a Catholic school. Even though we appreciated the gesture of the Catholics, it was not a good situation. The desks in the room were not large enough for adults. On several occasions the teacher in charge forgot to unlock the room for us. Needless to say, the morale of the congregation was lagging.

The inconvenience of meeting in the Catholic school spurred us to take action. The leaders drew up a simple plan. First, we started praying that God would open a way for us to build. Secondly, we started cleaning off the plot of land given to us by the city. Every Saturday morning, everyone, with the exception of those working on their jobs, came to work on the plot from 8.00am until 1.00pm.

An amazing transformation began to take place among the church people as we worked to clear the plot of land. In working together on the plot, we would laugh and talk together, sing the songs of faith and have a good time of fellowship.

I could see it on their faces, hear it in their voices and sense it in their attitudes. The church had a new vision. They believed that we were going to build our own church building. The positive action of clearing the plot of land rekindled the fires of faith.

We believed that we would build our own building. But where would we get the money to buy all the needed materials? Through the years the small congregation had deposited money in the bank for the building fund; however, devaluation had taken away most of its value. The church began to pray more fervently than ever before that the Lord would help us build a church for His glory.

One morning I telephoned our office in Lusaka. I happened to get John Garrison on the phone who was in Lusaka for an executive committee meeting. Having the church on my mind and heart, I shared with him our problem of not having enough money to build a church.

John said something that excited me: "Joe, we have special funds for putting up strategic buildings. Livingstone will qualify because it is the largest city in Southern Province. It certainly is in a strategic location."

Then, John added, "The executive committee is meeting now. If you can get the church leaders and members to write out their request and fax it here, you may get a response today. We finish up by 4.00pm, so you better hurry!"

Looking at my watch I saw that it was already 12.30pm. Racing out from the Post Office where I had called, I jumped in my truck and sped down to Clement Like's office. Like was the Chief Auditor for the government in Southern Province.

Catching him in his office I quickly explained what John Garrison had told me. Clement Like was decisive, "Let's draw up the paper here, then we'll go to the members."

By 3.00pm we had the signature of all the leaders and most of the members on the request. I faxed it to the executive committee in Lusaka. At 4.45pm I called Lusaka and talked to one of the executive committee members. He said that our request had been approved and money was immediately available for us to build our church. I went by Clement Like's office and told him the good news. We praised the Lord Jesus!

We went back to work on the plot with renewed energy and enthusiasm. Soon all the bushes and small trees were cleared away from where we wanted to construct the building. But alas, there was a huge tree in the very middle of the place where we wanted to build the church. Early in the morning ten of our men came with their axes. They took turns chopping on the thick trunk of the tree. In the middle of the afternoon, the tree came crashing down.

After their regular work hours and on Saturday morning, the men of the church came with their shovels and dug around the stump. Digging deep down around the stump, the men cut the roots attached to the stump. The digging left a deep, six-foot hole with a large stump in it. The challenge was to get the stump out of the hole. The church could not afford to rent a tractor or other machinery to extract the stump out of the hole.

I hooked onto the stump with my four-wheel drive truck and tried to pull it out, but I could not get any traction on the sandy soil. Several days later, a visiting missionary used his truck, along with mine, to try to pull the stump out. The stump did not budge. We were stumped!

As we stood looking at the stump in the hole, Clement Like summed up our situation: "We can't dig the foundation until this stump is taken out." Then, he added with a strong positive ring in his voice: "If we get this stump out, nothing can stop us from building!"

Waking up early the next morning (Saturday), I was thinking of how we could get the stump out of the hole. Then, it came to me clearly. Why had not I thought of it sooner? We needed leverage to get the stump out of the hole. After breakfast I drove to our plot. Most of the men had already arrived. They were standing around looking at the stump in the hole.

I told the men, "The stump is coming out this morning. We need eight long stout poles. You can cut them from the trees on the edge of our plot."

After a few minutes the men were back with the poles. I told the men to get in the hole and put the poles under the stump. I hooked onto the stump with a chain tied to my Toyota truck. I told them the plan: "When I pull forward with my truck, you come up with the poles. We'll inch the stump out."

It worked! Each time I gunned the truck and lurched forward, the men heaved up with the poles. Little by little, inch-by-inch we pulled the stump of the hole. The moment the stump cleared the hole, a loud cheer went up from all of us. It was a victory! Clement Like was dancing around and praising the Lord. He was shouting over and over, "Nothing can stop us now! Nothing can stop us now!"

Indeed, nothing stopped us. We built the Moise-O-Tunya Baptist Church. There were many other challenges along the way in building the church; however, none of them stand out like the time we were stumped. Whenever we see, or think about the Moise-O-Tunya Church, we are reminded that God will make a way, if we will trust Him and stay on course. Praise the Lord Jesus! He is able...

Reaching Out

Brother Moola, a deacon at the Moise-O-Tunya church, mentioned several times that he would like to see a new church started in the area where he lived. He came to our house to talk about us helping him start a new congregation.

He said, "There's ten thousand people in the Linda area and only a few churches with small congregations. The area needs a church that will evangelize and disciple new believers."

I told him, "Let's pray about this and come together in two weeks to talk further about it."

Two weeks later, Gloria and I met with Brother Moola and his wife, Beatrice. After we talked and prayed together, we set a date to start meeting together for Bible study and worship. Brother Moola would seek out a place for us to meet.

Permission was given for us to meet in the Linda Community Center. The Center was a spacious but run down facility in the very heart of the community. We would use one of the small rooms for our meeting place. Bible study and worship were scheduled for Sunday and Wednesday evenings. Five of us were present for the first meeting: Brother Moola, Beatrice, Gloria, Alice and myself. Alice was a Baptist from Choma. Her husband was not a believer.

I thought the work would grow quickly, but after two months we had added only one new believer. After six months we grew to twelve. I was disappointed. I had envisioned the church with at least fifty new believers by that time.

Some of our new members came from Maloni. Brother Moola did garden farming beyond Linda near the Maramba River. The village of Maloni was near by. He employed some of the Maloni people to work on his farm. While in the process of getting the Linda work started, we were making a lot of contacts in Maloni. They wanted us to start a church in their community.

While on a short furlough in the States, I invited the Haywood Baptist Association in Brownsville, Tennessee to come and hold evangelistic crusades. They agreed to come to Livingstone the following May.

As May approached, Brother Moola engaged every church member to help pass out flyers publicizing the coming crusade. The Linda area was saturated with news of our coming revival crusade.

Receiving permission from the Director of the Community Center, we whitewashed one sidewall of the Center for the showing of the Jesus film during the crusade.

In May 1993, Dr.Charles Pratt arrived from Brownsville, Tennessee, with a team of six men. They were ready to preach and to witness. The Zambians responded to their warm and engaging manner. We prepared for crusades, not only in Linda, but also in Maloni. We planned for two nights in Maloni and for three in Linda.

The first two nights we were in Maloni. I had never organized or held a crusade in Zambia, so I did not know what to expect. After the introductions and opening music, the lights were turned off. We showed the first roll of the Jesus film. Before the lights went off we had around two hundred people present. When the lights came back on, I was surprised to see around a thousand people.

Each night we averaged between eight hundred to a thousand people in attendance at Maloni. The opening introduction consisted of introducing team members, village dignitaries and explaining to the crowd what was going to take place.

Following the introduction, Abel Mwale led the crowd in some short choruses. Before the first roll of film was shown, there was special music. After the first roll of film was shown, one of the team members brought a short message that was interpreted by Brother Moola.

After the message, an invitation was given for those who wanted to make a commitment. Those who came forward were met by one of our counselors who gave them a Gospel of John and an appropriate tract. The counselors wrote down their names and addresses and assured them that a team would visit soon.

When the invitation was concluded, there was the showing of the second roll of the Jesus film.

At the conclusion of the Maloni crusade we had 235 people who made public commitments. We endeavored to follow up on every person who made a commitment to follow Christ as Lord and Savior.

The Linda crusade began the night after the Maloni crusade ended. Many of the Maloni people came to the Linda crusade, even though they had to walk three miles in pitch darkness to attend. We followed the same kind of program at Linda that we had at Maloni. The attendance at Linda averaged several thousand people each of the three nights. A total of 375 people made public commitments to follow Christ.

Our twelve follow-up teams started calling on those who made commitments the following morning after the first night of the crusade. The main work was to begin after the crusade was over. Every person was to be contacted and a clear presentation of the gospel given to them.

As a result of the Maloni Crusade, a church was started from those who professed Christ and were baptized.

A two-person team shared the plan of salvation with those who came forward in the crusade. If they wanted to be baptized and become a member of the church, they entered into a month long New Member's Class. If they completed the class, they were baptized.

The Maloni church now has more than two hundred members. Recent news from the area said that Maloni desperately needs more space to accommodate their growing attendance.

After the crusade in Linda, the church grew dramatically. We had to move from the small room that we were meeting in to the auditorium. The first Sunday following the crusade, we had more than a hundred people in attendance. Before that, we averaged fifteen and twenty people.

The most exciting and rewarding activities that we participated in, as missionaries, were to be catalysts in leading others to reach out. When a church is reaching out to touch others with the Gospel of Jesus Christ, it is an exciting and growing church.

Muyonga

We first heard about Muyonga from his wife, Alice. She was one of the charter members of the Linda Baptist Church. Each time we came together for Bible study and worship, Alice requested that we pray for Muyonga.

"He's lost and he makes life miserable for us because of his drinking problem," Alice explained to us.

Six months after we began meeting as a church we organized a revival/crusade. The crusade was held outside the community center. Three hundred and seventy five people made public commitments to follow Christ as Lord and Savior. Muyonga was one among those who made a commitment.

From following up those who made commitments in the crusade, ninety-five wanted to be baptized and become members of our church. However, only sixty-five enrolled in our baptism classes. Muyonga was among those who wanted to follow the Lord in baptism and become a member of Linda Baptist Church.

Brother Moola, our Pastor, taught the baptism class. The content of the teaching consisted of the meaning of baptism, the Lord's Supper and basic Christian beliefs. In order to be baptized and become a member of the church, each candidate was required to finish up the four consecutive sessions of the class.

On the Saturday following the second meeting of the baptism class, Brother Moola met me after the morning church visitation.

"Did you hear what Muyonga did last night?"

Without waiting for a reply, "He got drunk and and cursed out his neighbors."

Then, looking intently at me, he continued, "Would you

go with me to visit him? I'll have to tell him that he can't be in the Baptism class. We can't tolerate that kind of conduct."

I agreed to go with him.

Muyonga answered the door and politely received us. Brother Moola did all the talking. He just wanted me to come along to support him. He asked Muyonga if what he had heard about his drunken spree was true. Muyonga said that it was true. Then, he asked him if he was aware that this was a sinful, disgraceful and unacceptable act before the Lord and His people. Muyonga nodded in agreement with a contrite, sad look on his face. Brother Moola informed him that he could not continue as a member of the baptism Class. He nodded with head bowed without saying anything.

The next day, Sunday, I didn't expect to see Muyonga in church, but he was there. When Muyonga was sober he was a very polite and helpful person. He quickly volunteered to do any kind of repairs or work about the church meeting place. But when he was drunk he was ugly and abusive.

The second Sunday after Muyonga's getting expelled from the class, he came forward in the morning service. He told Brother Moola that he was repenting of his past sins and wanted to join the baptism class again.

That following afternoon Muyonga was re-enrolled in the Baptism Class. He lasted just a week. The following Saturday evening Muyonga got so drunk that he passed out on the path leading from the main market of the Linda community. The church people were really embarrassed.

Again, Brother Moola asked me to go with him to see Muyonga. There was the same speech from Brother Moola and the same look of contrition on the face of Muyonga.

That following Sunday Muyonga attended church. This time, he waited two weeks before he came forward again repenting of his sins and vowing to stay away from whisky and walk a straight path. Two weeks later Brother Moola agreed to let him enroll again in the Baptism Class.

Muyonga was the most knowledgeable member of the class. He knew all the answers. Not only was he intelligent, he studied diligently any materials given to him. He was quick to help other members of the class with their lessons. He was an excellent student to have in the class.

Muyonga was always polite and respectful toward the pastor, missionary and church leaders.

We were praying that he would claim the victory in the Lord Jesus Christ over his drinking problem.

But alas! This time Muyonga lasted three weeks before he fell before demon booze. He got drunk at home and had a brouhaha with his neighbors. It left Alice crying and despondent. We were also disappointed and saddened.

Once again, I went with Brother Moola to confront Muyonga about his shameful conduct. Muyonga seemed to be disgusted with himself. But I caught something new in his voice.

He vowed, "I'm going to overcome this with God's help!"

The next Sunday morning he came forward and told the congregation that he was tired of saying "yes" to his urge to drink.

He said, "I'm not able in my own strength to overcome this, but with the help and strength that Jesus gives me, I'll have victory over this shameful sin in my life. Please pray for me."

Some people thought that it was the same song and third verse. But there was a new determined commitment in Muyonga's voice and attitude.

Two weeks later Brother Moola re-enrolled Muyonga in the baptism class for the third time. He knew the class material as well as Brother Moola. Muyonga was probably the most learned baptismal candidate in all of Africa. He could quote the lessons from memory, and he often did in class.

This time Muyonga finished up the baptismal course. Two weeks later I had the privilege of baptizing him.

Muyonga became one of the leaders in the Linda Baptist Church.

If you have the opportunity to go to Livingstone, Zambia, visit the Linda community. While there, ask directions for going on to the Maloni community. After arriving in Maloni, and passing through to the far side, you'll see the Maloni Baptist Church sitting on a hill looking over toward Victoria Falls. This church has more than two hundred members. The pastor is Brother Muyonga.

He has a kind and helpful heart toward wayward lost sheep. But once they're saved, he has strong convictions about their being baptized!

Malaria in the Area

In our preparation for coming to Africa, we, somehow, did not get information on malaria. How we slipped up on this, I fail to understand. Malaria is endemic to Africa, especially to the areas around the Zambezi River. And it has been so for more than a hundred years.

During the time of David Livingstone, most of the missionaries and other foreigners who went to Africa, died from malaria and the complications from it. It was said that Africa was the graveyard for missionaries.

Until this day there are more than one million deaths each year resulting from malaria. The majority of these deaths are in Sub-Sahara Africa.

A few days after we arrived in Lusaka, we took John Mark to see a doctor. John complained of a sore throat and earache. The doctor tested him for malaria. We thought that was unusual, and even laughed about the strange way doctors practiced medicine in Zambia. We were not in the country very long before we realized the doctor knew exactly what he was doing.

Malaria can have multiple symptoms. It attacks the weaker parts of the body. It can be an ear, or throat. It usually starts with violent chills followed by intense fever and then profuse sweating. It is transmitted by the bite of a female anopheles mosquito.

Doctors know how important it is to treat malaria as soon as possible. Malaria left untreated, even for short period of time, can lead to cerebral malaria. Cerebral malaria often causes death.

We noticed that when missionaries came together in Africa for fellowship, the subject of malaria would inevitably come up. They would talk about the latest case of malaria in the family and what kinds of drugs were used to overcome it. There would be talk about the latest anti-malarial drug out on the market.

Why was this so? Malaria is part and parcel of living in Africa. Most missionaries and their family members suffer from one or more cases of malaria every year. Malaria affects their work and every area of life. Taking a prophylactic every morning is routine for many families.

On Christmas Day, 1990, I suffered from my first bout with malaria. I woke up at 4:00 a.m. feeling nauseated. After intense diarrhea, followed by chills and a high fever, I felt worse than I had ever felt in my life.

Just previous hours before, we had celebrated Christmas Eve with some Christian friends out in the country. Our daughter, Anne-Marie, and her friend, Wendy, were with us. They had just come in from the States. Both Anne-Marie and Wendy were nursing students at Samford University in Birmingham, Alabama.

Gloria was concerned and tried her best to get my fever down. Around 7.00am Anne-Marie and Wendy came to examine the patient. They showed some concern, but couldn't hide their elation at seeing their first malaria case. I overheard Anne-Marie tell Wendy, "Wait until we tell them about this! They'll not believe that we treated a malaria patient!"

At that time, we knew little or nothing about malaria. If we had studied up on it, we would have known that with the typical case of malaria, the fever will be intense and go up and down over a 12-hour period.

Since we didn't know the symptoms of malaria at the time, Gloria wanted to rush me to a hospital. My fever went down very little, even though I was taking Tylenol. On Christmas Day no doctors would be available in their
143

offices. The local hospital was the only option for emergency medical treatment.

With help, I managed to crawl in the back seat of our Toyota van. Gloria, Anne-Marie and Wendy took me to the provincial hospital. They half carried and dragged me to the waiting room where they checked me in. Even though it was Christmas Day, the waiting room was full of people. I slumped down on the bench feeling sicker than I could ever remember.

They called my name and a nurse led us to the examination room. She took my temperature and asked me questions that Gloria answered. Suddenly, I had to go to the bathroom. I was desperate!

I mumbled, "I've got to go to the W.C., bathroom, restrooms, whatever you call it! Where is it?"

The nurse calmly led me to the next room and put a bedpan on a table. The table was chest high. She said, "You can get on this table and use the bed pan. I'll pull the curtain."

Turning to Gloria I enunciated with all the strength that was left in me, "I couldn't get on that dumb table even if I was healthy."

Then, I took off down the hall seeking the restroom that is usually beside every waiting room. Fortunately, I found the restroom. It was in terrible condition, but I was too sick to care. It was in a worse condition when I left.

Returning to the examination room, the nurse led me in to be examined by the doctor. He was from Cuba and spoke broken English mixed with Spanish. I did not understand anything that he asked me. He poked around on my chest and stomach and then wrote out a prescription. It was for Chloroquine and Tetracycline. The nurse told Gloria that the doctor wanted me to come back at 3:00pm that afternoon.

Going out to get in the car, I told Gloria, "Get me home! I'm not coming back here ever. I'll die at home."

Despite my doubts about the doctor, I took the medicine as prescribed and recovered rather quickly. Three days later, we all left for Zimbabwe. We were taking Anne-Marie and Wendy to Sanyati Baptist Hospital where they would be doing a three-week internship with Dr. Maurice and Shirley Randall.

Despite the fact that we took a prophylactic every morning, Gloria and I, both, came down with malaria a number of times. During our five years in Livingstone, I had eleven cases of malaria and Gloria had seven. Undoubtedly, we lived in one of the worst malaria areas in Africa.

During our last year in Zambia, Gloria came down with a severe case of malaria. I gave her Fansidar and Tetracycline. After twelve hours, her fever did not break. Then, I started her on Halfan, a malaria drug from Egypt, along with Tetracycline. Still, after twelve more hours, her fever did not go down. I had been up with her for two days and nights. I took her to a doctor and he put her on quinine. Quinine is used as a last resort, because it has so many side effects. Shortly after Gloria began the quinine treatment, her fever broke and she recovered.

Before going to the doctor, we called several churches in the States and asked them to pray for Gloria. The call requesting prayer came on Wednesday afternoon, just before the Wednesday night prayer meeting. God did answer the prayers of His people. Whatever way He chose to do it, our Lord brought about Gloria's healing and complete recovery. We praise His name!

In thankfulness and praise to the Lord for her healing, Gloria planted border shrubbery plants on a bank just out-

side our front fence that spelled out the words: PRAISE
THE LORD JESUS.

For the next few months we enjoyed hearing Zambians
walk by and read the words aloud. Jesus was praised, and He
is worthy to be praised by every tongue, tribe and nation!

Rumors About My Pending Death

For about a month I had a low-grade fever. About four in the afternoon my fever would rise and last into the night. Thinking that it would go away, I did not visit a doctor. I lived a normal life, except that I was low on energy.

One day, acting upon the advice of Gloria, I went to the doctor. Livingstone was not the medical center of the world. As a matter of fact, if you came down with anything besides malaria or diarrhea, you needed to seek medical help somewhere else.

A new doctor had come to practice in Livingstone. He was of Indian ancestry and had, reputedly, studied at Oxford. I thought I would visit him.

The doctor was a small man weighing around a hundred and ten pounds and standing about five foot two inches tall. After examining me, he said in his British accent, "You have a parasite in your liver. I'm going to write you a prescription for flagell."

Arriving back home I vented my exasperation to Gloria. "I'm not going to these doctors again. They only prescribe the same medicines, no matter what kind of symptoms you have. Every time I go to one of these doctors I can predict what they are going to give me. It will be Chloroquine, Tetracycline, or Flagell."

Gloria advised, "Why don't you go to Lusaka or somewhere else?"

Thinking about what she said, I reached a decision. "I'm going to South Africa. The best medical treatment is available in Johannesburg. I'll call the Mission office in Lusaka and get permission."

After calling the mission office and getting permission, I called our mission office in Johannesburg and made reservations at the medical guesthouse. The hostess said that she would make an appointment for me to see the doctor that was used by the Mission.

Calling across the river to Victoria Falls City, I was able to make reservations for the 1:30pm flight. After packing my suitcase and eating a quick lunch, Gloria rushed me across the border in time to catch my flight.

My doctor's appointment was at 9.00am the following morning. The doctor was a tall, solemn-looking Afrikaaner. His nurse took, what I thought, was an inordinate amount of blood.

He told me to come back in two more days. Meeting my appointment after two days, I was ushered into the lab where the same nurse, again, took four vials of blood out of my arm. I began to feel like a pincushion!

During the time that I was in Johannesburg, Delos and Wanda Brown were there having their annual physical exams. The same doctor examined them. The doctor, knowing that I served in the same mission with Delos and Wanda, told them that he was concerned about the results of my blood tests. He said that he thought that I might have leukemia. He continued to say, "I'm making an appointment for Mr. Turman with a hematologist."

Delos and Wanda were concerned about my condition. They asked other missionaries to pray for me. Even though it was not confirmed, word quickly spread around that I had leukemia.

I was pleased when missionaries began to drop by my room and invite me out to dinner. They took me out to the best restaurants. Almost every day, before or around noon, a missionary would drop by and invite me. "A group of us are going out for dinner this evening, we would like for you to go with us."

Even though I had a low-grade fever in the evenings, I was having a great time. I did miss Gloria. Every morning I called to cheer her up. "Hey, hope all is going well. Yes, I'm doing great! Last night a group of missionaries took me out to this fabulous restaurant. We had a wonderful time trading missionary stories. The food was terrific. Guess what? This evening I've been invited to eat at a restaurant in a new mall. They say this mall makes those in America look pale in comparison. When am I coming home? I have an appointment with a hematologist next Thursday. I guess I'll just have to be patient and hold on until then. I do love you. I'll talk to you tomorrow."

I did manage to "hold on" until the following Thursday. In the meantime, I was taken on tours of the city by day and ate out in nice restaurants with new friends in the evening.

On a Sunday I had the opportunity of visiting Suweto. At that time, there was tension in the city because of the pending election. Early on Sunday morning I met a young man, a missionary journeyman, who was going to Suweto. He said that he worked with the Baptist church in that area, and he invited me to go with him. Worshiping with the Christians in Suweto proved to be the highlight of my South African trip.

On Thursday morning I had the appointment with the hematologist. As I sat in the waiting room, for the first time, I began to wonder if there was something seriously wrong with me. Why would I be examined by a hematologist?

Just as I was pondering these thoughts I was called into the doctor's office. The doctor was middle-aged, with a grave look on his face. When he stood to shake hands he did not smile or change expressions. His serious countenance only caused further concern about my tests. I sat facing him across a desk. He said nothing for some moments. It seemed like an eternity. My heart was racing. I thought: maybe there is something seriously wrong with me.

The doctor cleared his throat. He slowly looked up at me. Pronouncing my name with an Afrikaans accent, he said, "Mister Turman, you have a parasite in your liver. I'm going to write you a prescription for flagell."

Dazed, I stumbled out of his office. I did not know whether to laugh or cry. Deciding upon the former, I began to laugh loudly. I hee-hawed! People passing by must have wondered if I had escaped from an insane asylum.

The day after I arrived back home in Livingstone, I visited my Indian doctor friend. I had a new respect for him. Telling him my story we had a good laugh together. Before I left, he asked me about the dosage of the flagell prescription. When I told him what it was, he said, "It's not strong enough. Increase your dosage and you'll get well."

I followed his advice...and was soon back to normal health! Despite the rumors about my pending death, I'm still alive!

The Last Hectic Days in Zambia

A misunderstanding between the Baptist Mission of Zambia and the Zambian government caused a temporary suspension of work permits for Baptist missionaries. All of us whose work permits had expired were subject to being forced to leave the country.

The last six months in Zambia were hectic. Once every two or three weeks we were required to check in with immigration. During this time we thought that our work permits would surely be renewed and we would be able to stay in country. However each time we checked in with immigration, we would only be given a month or two weeks extension. This raised the stress level considerably, because we were unsure about our future.

There was some confusion about where we were to check in. Was it Lusaka or Livingstone? Since we lived in Livingstone, it seemed logical that we would report to immigration there. I did that; however, upon reporting, I was told that I had to go to Lusaka and report to immigration. Now, Lusaka was a good seven-hour trip over bad roads.

Gloria and I dutifully made the trip and reported to immigration in Lusaka. Alas! Immigration officials told us that we were to report to Livingstone immigration, not to Lusaka. We returned to Livingstone and reported to immigration. They were not happy to see us. It meant more work and trouble for them. The immigration officer told me to report to him every week.

The first week in February 1995, as I was making my weekly check in, the immigration officer told me that the chief immigration officer wanted to see me. Thinking that he had some good news about our work permits, I eagerly went into his office. He wasted no time in telling me the news; "Mr. Turman, you and your family must be out of Zambia by eight o'clock this evening."

Somehow, I thought I had misunderstood the chief immigration officer. I asked for confirmation. "You're saying that we are to be out of the country by eight o'clock this evening?" I asked incredulously.

He confirmed his previous statement. "Yes, you must be out of Zambia by eight o'clock tonight. If not, you will be arrested."

Knowing that it was impossible to get all of our household goods out in a few hours, I asked him, "Surely, we can come back and get all of our household goods, can't we?"

He shook his head negatively, "No, you can never come back."

Stumbling out of the immigration office, dazed by the news, I made my way home. Coming into the house, I told Gloria the news. Seeing the look of consternation on her face, I tried to reassure her. "I'll call the Baptist Mission office and they'll get our mission lawyer on this. There's no need to panic. We'll get this all straightened out."

I called our mission office and talked to Bonita Wilson, our administrator. She said, "Don't worry Joe! Our lawyer will get on this and take care of it." I called back around two o'clock. Bonita said that the lawyer was working on it. She would call when there was news.

In the meantime, we were making out a tentative list of things to take if we had to leave to get across the border by eight o'clock. At 4.45pm Bonita called to say that they had not been able to work out anything with immigration. We would have to leave. This left us very little time to get clothes, picture albums and valuables together to take across the border with us. There was no guarantee that we would be allowed to come back.

We had become friends with five Catholic nuns who lived several blocks from us. Two nights before we had them over for dinner and played board games. We called them and told them about our plight. They said they were coming over to escort us to the border. They volunteered to keep our dogs, or to do anything else that needed to be done. We asked them to pick up our mail at the post office. Richard, our security guard, would stay at the house and take care of the dogs.

At 7.00pm we left for the border. I was driving our Toyota truck. Gloria was driving our hatchback Mazda that we had bought from the Catholic sisters to be used in her ministry with the women. Both vehicles were fully loaded with everything we could pack in them. The Sisters followed behind us in their vehicle.

At 7.50pm we arrived at the border. We hugged the Sisters and quickly began to check through immigration. At exactly 8.00pm we checked into the Zimbabwe immigration line. We wondered if we would ever be allowed to return to get our household goods.

We spent the first two nights in Victoria Falls, Zimbabwe. Each day we called the Mission office in Lusaka to see if we could get back in the country. Bonita told us that it would take a while to get our work permit problem worked out with immigration. Realizing that we might be out of Zambia for an indefinite period of time, we went on up to Bulawayo, Zimbabwe.

In spite of our circumstances we enjoyed being in Bulawayo. Several Baptist missionary families lived there. We enjoyed having dinner and fellowship with these families. During the day, Gloria and I caught up on our reading and had prayer times together. We called in our telephone number to the mission office in Lusaka.

After ten days, we received a call from Lusaka telling us that immigration promised to grant us permission to re-enter Zambia and get our household goods. The granting of permission was imminent, so we needed to position ourselves in Victoria Falls to be ready to cross the border. Early the next morning we left for Victoria Falls. After spending two nights in Victoria Falls, we were given permission to return to Livingstone. Immigration gave us a month to pack up and settle up all of our business. A hectic month was behind us and an uncertain month lay ahead.

The Last Trip to Lusaka: A Nightmare

The last month in Livingstone was spent in finalizing our time with the churches and packing our household goods. The churches would keep on going without us. They were self-supporting, self-governing and self-propagating. We had worked with the churches as catalysts to get new programs and churches started. Often, we were the contact persons to get literature and other needed materials to the churches. The church leaders called upon us to help in training the membership.

We organized a garage sale the third week of the last month. Missionaries, expats and Zambians flocked to our house to buy our household goods. We kept some essentials for setting up a house, in case we could return to Zambia.

One of the vacationing missionary families from Lusaka dropped the mission truck off at our house as they were passing through Livingstone. We loaded it with our remaining household goods and stretched a tarp over it.

The morning of our departure, a number of our Zambian friends came to say goodbye. They really thought they would see us back soon. We, ourselves, thought that we would be back in a matter of months.

Before we left Livingstone, we called the Baptist Mission office and told them that we anticipated arriving in Lusaka between 4.00 and 5.00pm.

I drove the mission truck loaded with our household goods. Gloria drove our Toyota truck packed with our personal belongings.

Not able to find suitable owners for our two dogs, we took them with us. I had Jake, our Rottweiler, with me. Gloria had Wendy, our Maltese poodle, with her in the small truck. We expected to find homes for them in Lusaka.

The first town that we passed through was Kalomo. I remembered the crusade that we held on the city square in Kalomo. Wade Coker, a fellow Baptist missionary, helped share with the preaching. From the dozens of people who made commitments, a church was organized and is still functioning in Kalomo.

Leaving Kalomo we traveled twenty-five miles on to Choma. A large, sprawling city, Choma was the Tonga capital. We worked frequently with the Choma Baptist Church. They were a small struggling group who met in a school building. On two different occasions we held crusades in Choma. They were well attended and lifted the morale and attendance for the local churches.

While we were getting gas at a service station in Choma, we saw a car with a broken windshield. An Indian lady, one of the passengers in the car, stuck her head out the side window and asked Gloria where were we going. Gloria told her that we were going to Lusaka. She emotionally exhorted, "No, no, you cannot go to Lusaka today! There are riots in Mazabuka and they're targeting foreigners. See! Our windshield is broken. We barely made it out of the city."

Upon hearing this sobering news, Gloria and I discussed our next move. We decided to go on to Monze, the town some thirty miles from Mazabuka. There, we would check with the police about the situation in Mazabuka. If it wasn't safe, we would spend the night in Monze.

Arriving in Monze, we checked with the police and were informed that there were still riots in Mazabuka. We asked them about a hotel to spend the night. They told us how to get to their largest and best hotel. Driving up to the hotel we quickly saw that we could not spend the night there. A rowdy nightclub was just next door to the hotel, and even though it was just getting dark, noisy and rambunctious activities had already started.

I waved for Gloria to follow me and drove to a large Catholic church that we had passed in coming through the town. The church had a large compound behind it with a number of buildings and apartments. One of the night guards let us in. The guard told us that one of the sisters was in charge of the accommodations.

Gloria asked the sister if we could spend the night in the compound. They had no room, but she knew of a white farmer who lived eight miles out in the country who enjoyed entertaining out of town guests. She called him and he invited us to come on out.

This arrangement sounded great; however, there was one problem. It was the rainy season, and once you get off the tarmac, and get on dirt roads you have a problem with a large loaded truck. We came four miles down the dirt road leading to the farmer's house. There facing us in the middle of the road was a large puddle of water some ten yards wide. The large Japanese made truck that I was driving had no four-wheel drive. I knew that if I got stuck we would be there for the night.

There was no place to turn the truck around. We had to back our trucks out some two miles before we could find a place to turn around.

By that time, it was almost midnight. We headed back to the Catholic compound. Arriving back at the compound, we asked the guards if we could spend the night in the compound sleeping in our trucks. Sleeping? Have you ever tried sleeping in the cab of a truck with a large dog?

As tired as I was, I was not able to get one wink of sleep. When I tried to let Jake out of the cab, he frightened the guards so much that I had to get him back in.

Getting out of my truck, I noticed that Gloria was not getting much sleep. We decided to leave at 3.30am and try to get through Mazabuka before the rioters were awake. As we approached Mazabuka I put the pedal to the metal. We came roaring right through the middle of Mazabuka! Gloria was just behind me.

We saw only one person. He was a young man, and when he saw us, he reached down and picked up a rock. I prayed, "Lord, don't let him throw it! Don't let him throw it!" My truck had an enormous windshield. It would have splattered all over the place. The young man juggled the rock from one hand to the other, but did not throw it. Praise the Lord!

Heading on for Lusaka we met Fred Allen and Jim Cook who came looking for us. They had heard on the news about the riots in Mazabuka. When we did not show up in Lusaka, they were concerned about us. We were glad to see them!

After spending two days in Lusaka finalizing with the Baptist Mission, we caught a flight out to the USA.

Africa will always have a special place in our hearts.

Responding to His Call

A casual reading of the Book of Acts shows that the Apostle Paul and his companions moved from place to place under the leadership and guidance of the Holy Spirit. Acts 13:2 states clearly that Paul and Barnabas were called out and sent by the Holy Spirit to become the first cross-cultural missionaries.

There are many aspects to being called out to be missionaries. The mind, will and emotions are all involved. No two missionaries have the same experience. Salvation experiences all differ. In the same way, missionaries have differing experiences in their calling. The need of the country, the personnel in the country, the kinds of ministries available, and the emphasis of the mission in a particular country are all factored into the commitment made by a missionary.

But the bottom line is the leadership of the Holy Spirit in a missionary's calling. He is the One who calls and sends.

While we were on furlough in 1995-96, we began to think about another place of service. Since Zambia had closed to us, we looked at other countries in Africa. Dr. John Faulkner sent us ten job descriptions for church planters to serve in areas of South Africa, Lesotho, Swaziland and Namibia.

But as we prayed about these invitations, we did not feel a sense of rightness about returning to Africa. Even though we enjoyed our years of ministry in Zambia, we did not have a sense of God's leadership in returning to that great continent.

After saying "no" to Africa, we had calls from Southeast Asia inviting us to return to Indonesia. Our oldest son, Joey, and his family, lived in Jakarta. We speak the

Indonesian language. It seemed logical that we would return to Indonesia.

Yet, as we prayed about returning to Indonesia, we simply did not feel the leadership of the Holy Spirit to return to that beautiful country. We, again, said "no."

Saying "no" the second time to areas of the world that we were familiar with left us feeling drained and isolated.

I said to Gloria, "We're going to be put out to pasture. We've said no to the only two areas of the world that we've served in."

We had been in frequent communication with the International Mission Board about possible countries for a ministry. Feeling tired from all the processes, I wearily declared, "We'll not call anymore. If the Lord wants us to go to another country, He'll have to stir someone's heart to call us."

After that pronouncement, we had prayer together on the sofa. I don't remember all of our prayer, but I do remember us praying that we were ready and willing to go wherever God wanted us to go. I do remember clearly my concluding sentence in the prayer: "Lord, if You have something for us, have someone to call us."

Just as I said "Amen," the telephone rang. Gloria and I looked at each other. She answered the phone. "Yes, just a moment please."

Then, putting her hand over the receiver, "You're not going to believe this!"

It was Roger Briggs from the Central Europe office. He wanted to know if we were interested in going to Bratislava, Slovakia, to serve as pastor and wife of the International Baptist Church. He made it clear that this position was to be used to start new missions and churches in the area. A surge of excitement swept over me.

Immediately, I felt a sense of rightness about this opportunity. But we needed to spread this out before the Lord. I told Roger that we would pray about it and get back with him as soon as we knew something.

After hanging up, I shared with Gloria all that Roger had shared with me about Bratislava. She also became excited about the prospects of living and serving in Slovakia.

Five days later we called Roger and told him that we felt right about going to Slovakia.

After making this commitment, we felt at peace about it. As we began to make preparations for going to Slovakia, we felt a sense of God's leadership.

Our children shared in our excitement about going to a new part of the world. Our two older were already married, and the two younger were in college.

Although we had served in four countries over a twenty-eight-year span, we still felt a sense of joy and excitement about our new mission. It was almost like going out for the first time. This joy, we knew, came from the Holy Spirit. He called us to serve in a new area of the world and as we responded in obedience, He filled us with joy.

Building Bridges in Bratislava

Arriving in Bratislava on 5 September 1998, we were met by Craig Averill who took us to the twelve-story apartment building where we would be living on the eleventh floor. Craig and, his wife, Glenda, were studying the Slovak language. We would be the only two Baptist Missionary couples serving in Slovakia.

Going up to the eleventh floor we met the pastor and wife that we would be replacing. Ben and Meredith Hannah were pastor and wife of International Baptist Church of Bratislava. They were in their middle twenties, and had led the church during the past two years in a creative ministry. Leaving early the next morning, they were returning to their hometown in Texas.

After leaving most of our baggage in the apartment, we spent the night with Craig and Glenda. Early the next morning we moved into our apartment. The church rented out the apartment for the pastor and his family. It was small by American standards, yet comfortable enough for a couple. It became our home for the next few years.

Our congregation was, indeed, international. Usually, eight or ten nationalities attended Sunday worship services. They blended together very well in a common desire to worship and serve Christ the Lord. The members of the church consisted of embassy personnel, international schoolteachers, businessmen and their families, students from different countries, and nationals from Slovakia.

The use of English in the worship service limited the number of Slovaks who attended.

One of the Slovaks who attended was Peter Stefek. Peter, in his late twenties, worked for a computer company. He came to experience Christ in his life under Ben

Hannah's ministry. Peter wanted to be baptized in the same lake in Switzerland where Zwingli was baptized. This presented a problem, as he did not know anyone in Switzerland, much less anyone who would baptize him.

The way opened up for him just after Christmas 1996. Ben Hannah was going to Interlaken, Switzerland, for a retreat after Christmas. Peter would meet Ben at the lake just outside of Zurich.

Not having the money for an airfare Peter hitchhiked to Zurich. Peter enjoyed telling the story of his trip and the many adventures he encountered along the way. One night he slept under a bridge along the highway. Several times, the Lord brought just the right people into his life to provide for him. He would say several times during his story: "God took care of me. I wasn't afraid. I was trusting Him and doing what He wanted me to do."

Ben did baptize Peter in Lake Zurich. Peter said that the cold water did not bother him, but Ben almost froze to death.

It was Peter who introduced me to my first computer. He never called me pastor or reverend rather he called me "Sjoe," putting a special accent to it. For weeks Peter kept saying to me, "Sjoe, you need a computer. It will save you time. You can do your work so much more efficiently. Sjoe, I will teach you how to use it."

Finally, just before Christmas I told Peter to get me a computer for the best price. He assured me that he would get what I needed for the best price. He did just that, and came three hours each week to teach me the fundamentals of how to use a computer.

I will always be grateful to Peter for getting me started on computers.

Gloria made a lot of contacts as she rode the trolley from our area of the city to downtown. Since we had served in Africa and Asia we could identify with people from those continents. Gloria met African students on the trolley and invited them to attend our worship service. These contacts led to a number of African students attending our church.

One of the students was Blessing from Nigeria. His enthusiasm and love for the Lord Jesus was contagious. He and a friend came to our apartment one day. He said to me, "Pastor, may I speak frankly to you about our worship service?"

"Yes, please do, Blessing. I'm open to hear you."

"Pastor, our worship, well, it does not have enough life. It needs the life that comes from the Holy Spirit's anointing on the service. This anointing comes when we really pray and seek God's face."

Listening to what Blessing said, I could not find anything wrong with his statement. "Yes, we always need the life that comes from the Spirit's anointing, Blessing. What do you propose that we do?"

"Pastor, we need to form a band of pray-ers, those who really want to pray. Back in Nigeria we call them 'The Prayer Warriors Band.' We could meet on Saturday to pray for the Sunday worship service and other activities."

Knowing that prayer is always needed I nodded in agreement. "Blessing, we'll need someone to lead the Prayer Warriors Band. We'll need someone who really believes in the power of prayer."

I was trying to think who could lead this program. Yes, of course, Blessing could lead it. No one is more interested in praying than Blessing.

"Blessing, I have just the right person to lead this praying band."

"Who's that Pastor?"

"Blessing, I want you to lead the Prayer Warrior's Band! Would you do it?"

"Yes, Pastor, I will do it."

Those of us who were interested in praying for the church and its activities met on Saturday afternoons. We were a small band, but we had the most spirited prayer meetings that I've ever been in.

In order to contact more internationals, we started a Saturday evening program that met once every two months called "The International Fun and Fellowship." Most of these programs featured music from different countries, recognizing each country represented and those from that country, special music, and a five-minute devotional followed by refreshments. Sometimes, we had Christian drama groups to bring the main program.

We publicized the program every way possible. It was on local radio stations and in the newspaper. But most people came because of the leaflets that were handed out by members of our congregation. From the beginning, the program was well attended. Half of those who came were new contacts for our church.

A Christmas Eve in Bratislava

It was Christmas Eve, and the weather was cold, brutally cold. We could look out from our eleventh floor apartment windows and see people trudging about all bundled up like Eskimos.

Gloria had come down with a light case of flu with fever and a hacking cough. She would not be getting out in the cold.

I was to lead in the Christmas Eve service. It was to be a traditional candle light service. I would start with that and plan any kind of program that could be related to the candle light service.

It had been a fast and furious week that had left no time to plan for a Christmas Eve service. Thankfully, I had this free afternoon to plan a program. I wrote out a drama that had ten speaking parts. The parts were short and could be read...if there was enough light.

I was worried about who would be the main speaker in the drama. The other small parts could be handled quite easily. But the longer part...it could be a problem getting someone this late. Most people would not want to take a part of that length without some preparation. This part would guide and give life to the entire drama. It needed someone who was spontaneous and could breathe life into it.

Darkness was falling as I bathed and got ready to leave for the service. I tried to cheer up Gloria, who would be left by herself for a long evening. "Gloria, you have the better part: to stay in this warm apartment and pray for the service. You would not want to be outside. It's five degrees with fifteen degrees below zero chill factor. We will miss you. Wish you could go."

The candles were stored in a closet in our apartment. I was to bring them with matches. Carefully, I placed them in our shopping bag and stuffed old newspapers over them. Lifting up the shopping bag, I was surprised at their weight. I would have to lug these candles with me, first, on the bus, and then take a trolley to the building complex where we met in one of the auditoriums.

Gloria looked anxiously at the clock, "You better give yourself plenty of time to get there. Public transport may be slow this evening."

"I'll leave at six as the program starts at seven. That should give me enough time to get there and get ready."

I dressed as warmly as possible and left the apartment to catch the bus which stopped just in front of our apartment. I had tried to time the arrival of the bus by looking out the apartment window at the buses, and the interval of time that lapsed before the next one came. They came and went at fifteen-minute intervals.

When the 5.45pm bus left, I gave myself ten minutes to maximize time spent in the warm building. Then, I caught the elevator down to the first floor and quickly headed for the bus stop.

Going out the door I was met by a blast of cold air, colder than I had ever experienced.

Standing at the bus stop, I eagerly looked and listened for the coming bus. At six there was no bus. Ten minutes after six and still no bus. I could feel the cold penetrating my clothing, so I retreated back to the apartment building lobby. I could look out the long front window and see the bus when it approached the stop. If there were a number of passengers to board the bus, one would have time to run from the lobby to the bus stop and board. But there were no passengers in sight. I could not chance it. I had to be there to lead the program.

Knowing that I couldn't afford to miss the next bus, I rushed back to the bus stop. It was another cold ten minutes before the bus came.

The bus took me a mile down the hill to the trolley line. There, I would catch a trolley that would take me to the front of the building which housed our auditorium.

Getting off at the trolley line, I noticed that there was only one passenger waiting to catch a trolley. I would not be here, I thought, if I was not the pastor going to lead a service. It's too cold for man or beast. Besides that, I was thinking, only a few people will get out in this weather. I will be surprised if we have ten people. If we have three or four people, we'll just have prayer together and go home.

The trolley was late, also. By the time it arrived I was cold as a popsicle. Never had I been so cold! Getting on the trolley, I noticed that it was 6.45pm. The trolley made good time because there were so few passengers to get on and off. We arrived in front of our building at 6.55pm.

Hurrying off the trolley, I rushed up the steep steps of the building complex to the second floor where we met in our auditorium. I wanted to be on time, even if two or three people were waiting.

Stepping inside the auditorium, I was shocked! I stood there holding the bag of candles speechless. "Pastor, are you all right? Merry Christmas!"

"Yes, yes, I'm O.K. Merry Christmas!"

The auditorium was packed! People were sitting on the floor because there were not enough chairs, and more people were streaming in the door.

Coming to my senses, I knew I had to move quickly to get ready for the program. Peter and Steve would give everyone a candle. We had a hundred candles. Eighty-five people were present. Moving around the auditorium, I handed out the short parts for the drama.

Who would take the main part, the most important speaking role? Mark, yes. He could do it. Where is he? I was desperately looking for Mark. He was not in the auditorium. Just then, the door opened and another group of people entered the auditorium to further pack it out. Mark was among them! You couldn't miss him. He always wore Bermuda shorts. He had them on, but with a coat. Yes, he grew up in Alaska.

After greeting the group and meeting each of Mark's friends, I called Mark over to the side and asked him if he would take the main speaking part. "Mark, you can make this come alive. You're the one for this part! Will you do it?"

"No problem, Pastor. I'll do it."

Even to this day I have not experienced a worship service like that one. We began singing Christmas carols and a reverent hush and awe settled over the Christmas Eve crowd. Was it because most of us were far away from our homeland? Or was it because of the brutally cold weather? Yes, these could have been factors in how we bonded that evening. But in the main, it was the Spirit of Him who was born that first Christmas night in Bethlehem, that united us together in such a warm and loving fellowship.

After the singing and prayers of thanksgiving and praise, we had our drama that preceded the lighting of the candles. The drama was presented as if the participants had practiced it for days.

Mark was simply superb. The drama came alive as he masterfully spoke his part with feelings that expressed love and compassion.

After the drama, we had the traditional candle lighting as we sang "Silent Night." In the dim candlelight, tears glistened on many cheeks. Some wept softly.

Yes, Christ came that night to a most unlikely place, Bratislava, Slovakia, and to a most unlikely people, a group of foreigners meeting together in an auditorium. But He came with the most joyful word that He has come to save us from our sins and to give us eternal life.

That first Christmas Eve in Slovakia will always live in my memory and heart because Christ met with us in such a real and powerful way.

Taking a Leap of Faith

During the spring of 1998, Gloria and I decided that it was time to reap from the seeds planted from the previous International Fun and Fellowship meetings. We presented the plan to the church of having an International Fun and Fellowship meeting with music and drama, but closed out with a strong evangelistic message and appeal. The previous programs had five to ten minutes of Gospel presentation, but no invitation.

Most of the congregation was excited about the possibilities of a program that would have a strong evangelistic appeal, however, some doubted. The doubters said that invitations were not given in the context of the Slovak culture. They were afraid that an evangelistic appeal would be misunderstood and drive away the people that we had cultivated in the previous programs.

Gloria and I plunged ahead in preparing for the International Fun and Fellowship program. We would need quality Christian music and a speaker that could relate to those less than thirty years of age.

As we began to pray for the program, along with the church, we felt led to invite a well-known choir from one of the local Baptist churches to bring the main music. The choir of thirty consisted mainly of young people. The choir leader, V. Kral, was an energetic leader who knew how to inspire and motivate his choir.

After inviting the choir, we knew we could have a space problem if we used the same auditorium that we used for worship. The auditorium that we met in for worship could hold seventy people. It would be crowded with that number of people. If we had the attendance that we anticipated, we would need to rent another auditorium for the Saturday night program.

Now, we had to convince the church to go along with us renting another auditorium for one night. In making the case, I told the congregation that we would surely have more than a hundred to attend the program. Someone mentioned that our previous Saturday night programs had only fifty or sixty in attendance. Why rent a larger auditorium when we had one that could accommodate up to seventy people?

Somehow I knew we would have our largest crowd, so I took the leap of faith. "We'll have more than a hundred for the program. A larger auditorium will be necessary to accommodate them."

The congregation went along with getting a larger auditorium. Some people had skeptical looks on their faces, but praise the Lord, were willing to try it.

I went on with the planning refusing to consider the "what if..." Even though it is difficult to get people in Bratislava to attend a Saturday night program sponsored by a church, I, somehow, knew that it was going to happen.

We did all pray harder and work more than we did in preparation for the previous programs. Blessing got his Prayer Warriors going in prayer. The program began to come into focus.

Now, we had to get the right speaker. We needed someone who could relate to the majority of those in attendance who would be thirty years and younger. Josh Smith came to my mind. Josh served with a Para-church group who worked among the youth in Slovakia. He was strong in the Word and had a winsome smile and engaging personality. I contacted him, and he could be our speaker.

The night of the program I came early to check out the auditorium to see that all was in place. Several of our young professionals volunteered to help out with showing people how to get to the auditorium, which was on the second story of the large complex.

The program was to start at 7:00pm. At 6:50pm I met Steve Watt in the large lobby where I was standing to greet and direct people to the meeting place. Steve was helping as an usher. He had just come from the auditorium. "Steve, how many people do we have?"

Steve with a look of concern on his face, "Pastor, we only have about fifteen."

"We still have ten minutes, Steve. Let's see what happens." After speaking to Steve, I went to meet a couple from our congregation. They introduced me to some friends that they had brought to the program.

After speaking with several more friends, I went to the auditorium. I could hardly believe my eyes! In those ten incredible minutes something wonderful had happened! The auditorium had filled up so that there was standing room only. The ushers spotted me and came rushing to me.

"Pastor, what are we going to do? We don't have enough chairs."

"Hey, grab some of your friends and bring chairs down from our regular meeting place." They scurried off to get extra chairs.

The program went wonderfully well. The music, the personal testimonies, and the message were all translated into the Slovak language from English. The Spirit of the Lord permeated the auditorium. Josh had the anointing of God's Spirit as he shared a simple but powerful message on the meaning of the cross.

We gave an invitation to those who wanted to come and publicly profess Christ as Lord and Savior. Seven Slovaks came to openly confess Christ as Lord and Savior.

Later on, one of the Slovak young people said to me, "We have never experienced a worship service like this! This service has touched all of our lives. We'll never be the same because we were here tonight."

That experience only confirmed to me that God is seeking and yearning for the salvation of those who are lost to Him. He is longing and willing to work with His people to bring others into a right relationship with Himself through the finished work of His Son, Jesus Christ, on the cross.

Goodbye and Hello

The years have gone by so quickly! Now, it is time to say goodbye to Slovakia and foreign mission work. It is time for official retirement. But we will never retire from service in the Lord's Army. Retirement means saying hello to another chapter in our lives.

This new chapter has already been opened, and, so far, it has been exciting. It has been fun getting adjusted to life in America. After all, we served thirty years overseas. The America that we have returned to is so different from the America that we left in 1969.

Retiring, for us, means freedom to enter new doors of ministry. It means going on mission trips to countries that we have never visited. It means getting involved in the many multifaceted ministries here in the States. Retirement gives us time to get involved with the local church and association programs.

But we want to stay in the main stream of missions. For that reason we participate in eight to ten On Mission Celebrations a year with the International Mission Board, of the SBC. This gives us an opportunity to touch base with churches all over America.

Upon retiring, we wanted to revisit the countries that we had formerly served in as missionaries. That desire had been partially realized as we have visited Vietnam and Indonesia.

Going back to Vietnam in January 1999, after twenty-four years, was especially meaningful for us. In preparation for the trip, we prayed that the Lord would lead us in making contacts with Vietnamese Christians that we had served with in the years 1969-75.

It was an emotional moment for us as Air Vietnam touched down at Tan Son Nhut airport. We remembered vividly the day we last left from this airport on 1 April 1975.

We checked in a small hotel not far from the Grace Baptist Church. As it was Saturday evening, we asked the Christian couple who operated the hotel about the time of church services at Grace. They advised, "The services start at 6.30am, but you need to go early to find a seat."

Getting up early the following morning, we caught a taxi to church. The church was already full, except for a few seats. During the worship service there was standing room only. After the sermon was delivered, an invitation was given. Four adults came forward to publicly confess Jesus Christ as Savior and Lord. Following the worship service, sixteen adults were baptized.

Early Monday morning we took a bus to Dalat. Our oldest son, Joey, our daughter-in-law, Stephanie, and our granddaughter, Kaitlin, accompanied us. Walter and Pauline Routh, our fellow missionaries from Vietnam days of service, were also on the bus. They were going to a small town near Dalat to work on a water project.

Arriving in Dalat in the early afternoon, we had lunch and checked in our hotel. Later that evening after dinner, we walked around the Dalat Lake to check out the lobby of the Dalat Palace Hotel. The French built the hotel in the 1920s. A French company had just finished renovating it. Several people in Saigon told us to be sure and see the uniquely decorative lobby of this famous landmark in Dalat.

As we were walking through the lobby of the Dalat Palace Hotel, something happened that can only be described as a supernatural experience. As I was walking some ten steps behind my family, I heard the sound of a piano. Instantly, the face of Anh Hien came to my mind and heart.

During our time of serving in Nha Trang, Anh Hien was the youth leader for the church. He, also, was our church musician as he played five instruments.

Stopping, I turned around and began to follow the sound of the piano. Walking down a narrow hallway, I turned left to follow the sound of the piano. The hallway ended at the door of a restaurant. Entering the restaurant, I could still hear the piano, but could not see it.

Turning a corner I saw the piano and a man hunched over the keyboard. Approaching to get a closer look, I recognized the man as Anh Hien. He was older to be sure, but it was he!

Walking up to the piano, I said, "Anh Hien, I am Missionary Joe Turman."

Anh Hien stood up with a startled and surprised look on his face. He finally managed to say, "It is you after all these years!"

We hugged one another.

I took Anh Hien to the lobby to meet the rest of the family.

The following two mornings we met Anh Hien for breakfast and lunch. He shared with us about his experiences over the past twenty-four years. Even though he had suffered some difficult times, he was positive about his life in Vietnam.

In sharing about past difficult experiences, he would end up saying, "Now, that is behind me. Our life is good now. My wife and two teenagers are doing well. We are living a good life."

Anh Hien gave us the addresses of our Christian friends in Nha Trang. Two days later we took a bus down to Nha Trang and made contact with our friends that we had not seen since April 1975. We had a wonderful reunion!

We are grateful to the Lord that he allowed us to meet these dear Christian friends after so many years.

We are still "getting on with the going!" We are still on mission! Whatever the Lord Jesus has for us, we want to live and serve in the mainstream of His will and purpose. We want to live for His honor and glory. Praise His name!

ORDER FORM

Qty.	Title	Price	Total
	Getting On With The Going	$12.00	
		Sub-Total	
		+S&H*	
		Total	

*S&H: Add $2.00 shipping and handling for the first book and $1.00 for each additional book.

Purchase this book by ordering from:

Joe Turman
396 Bethel Church Road
Guntersville, AL 35976

Tel. 256-571-4253 or
E-mail: joeturman@bellsouth.net